Water Gardening
❧ B A S I C S ❧

Water Gardening
B A S I C S

Helen Nash & Marilyn M. Cook

Sterling Publishing Co., Inc.
New York

Designed by Judy Morgan

Library of Congress Cataloging-in-Publication Data

Nash, Helen, 1944–
    Water gardening basics / Helen Nash & Marilyn M. Cook.
        p. cm.
    Includes index.
    ISBN 0-8069-5747-6
    1. Water gardens. I. Cook, Marilyn M. II. Title.
    SB423.N38   1999
    635.9'674--dc21   99-11932
                                            CIP

1 3 5 7 9 10 8 6 4 2

Published by Sterling Publishing Company, Inc.
387 Park Avenue South, New York, N.Y. 10016
© 1999 by Helen Nash
Distributed in Canada by Sterling Publishing
℅ Canadian Manda Group, One Atlantic Avenue, Suite 105
Toronto, Ontario, Canada M6K 3E7
Distributed in Great Britain and Europe by Cassell PLC
Wellington House, 125 Strand, London WC2R 0BB, England
Distributed in Australia by Capricorn Link (Australia) Pty Ltd.
P.O. Box 6651, Baulkham Hills, Business Centre, NSW 2153, Australia
Printed in China

Sterling ISBN 0-8069-5747-6

Additional photo credits
page 2: H. Nash; page 3: Perry D. Slocum; pages 5-7, 9-11, 27, 45, 52, 68: H. Nash; page 76: Bob Romar, courtesy of Maryland Aquatic Nursery; page 90: Ron Everhart; page 90 (bottom left): courtesy of Tetra Second Nature; pages 122-123: H. Nash

*To all who dream of personal, private havens
outside their own back door, and to the warm friends
who open their hearts and gardens to us.*

*And to Joe Cook, cherished husband
and brother-in-law.*

Contents

❧

Introduction

$\mathcal{A}$sk pond owners why they installed a water garden or fish pond in the backyard, and one answer predominates: for the peace and tranquility. In our modern day of concrete, stress, and daily changes, one thing in our world remains steadfast—the attraction of water. We vacation at the beach. We build a second home at the shore. We buy a new home in a subdivision rife with ponds and spouting fountains. The sound of water, the reflections upon it, and the life within it soothe our souls and frazzled nerves.

Most pond owners, too, admit that water gardening is addictive. The first pond is never big enough and one pond is never enough. But digging a hole in the yard is a commitment. It's not like trying out a new variety of petunia. Water gardeners often joke that the commitment rapidly becomes a passion, finally evolving into absolute obsession. The key to turning a commitment into an obsession is success.

Because there are many different ways to do the deed, success is ensured by learning as much as possible before lifting the first shovelful of dirt. Your lifestyle and time will determine your parameters. A swimming pool sand filter, for example, will work in a backyard pond, but will require daily backwashing. If you're home all day, every day, playing in your yard, such high maintenance may not faze you. Most of us, however, wish for less work and much more aesthetic enjoyment!

This book will arm you with a broad base of information to ensure you of successful *water-gardening experiences. But don't stop here! Read as much as you can, question it all, and talk to other water gardeners. You may be surprised to learn that a pond club of experienced water gardeners and fishkeepers is nearby. Water gardeners are an enthusiastic lot —quick to share our love of the life in our waters. Whether you seek out each other or simply bask in the quiet tranquility of your own creation, you will find your pond a source of year-round pleasure, joy, and peace... all within your own backyard haven. Enjoy!*

Helen Nash and Marilyn Cook

CHAPTER ONE

Planning Your Water Garden

Natural ponds provide inspiration for the smaller, closed systems we create in our backyards.
Photo by H. Nash

WHAT KIND OF POND DO YOU WANT?

A water garden is much more than just a hole in the ground. It is an artificially constructed, usually lined, "closed" ecosystem that mimics natural water features. What you intend to put in a pond and how that pond will fit within your landscape determine how you will build it. As you plan your pond, remember that you don't have to build it all at once. Developed in stages, a water feature grows with your vision and experience, as well as extends its cost over a manageable period of time.

Ponds for Fish

Fish are part of the fascination of a water garden. Besides adding life and color to the garden, they perform a vital function—they eat mosquito larvae!

Space

Fish do grow. A two-inch-long goldfish may end up being 9 or 10 inches long in two years. A four-inch-long koi may end up being 22 inches long in the same time! Generally plan on an inch of fish per square foot of water surface, or an inch of fish per five gallons of water volume. Some experts recommend that the figure be halved for koi. (If you plan a pond that will measure six feet by eight feet, you could then plan to have 48 inches of fish eventually—or 24 inches of koi.) This general guide is known as the *fish stocking level* of the pond. Whichever stocking-level guideline you follow, the closer you come to

Learning the Language

aeration—the action of air bubbling into the pond water, which allows oxygen to enter the water

biofilter—a chamber containing media that provide a home for nitrifying bacterial growth, which enhances the natural nitrogen system of the pond and promotes good water quality

closed ecosystem—a self-contained system that does not rely on nature to supply its needs; in water gardening, an artificially constructed system managed by the pondkeeper

cold-water fish—fish that survive in waters that chill to below 50° F, usually with at least occasional ice coverage. Koi and goldfish are the usual pond fish of this type.

drainage ditch—a channel dug into the ground, which is then filled with rocks and a perforated drainage tile at the bottom to collect ground water and direct it elsewhere

fish load—how many inches of fish or, more generally, the number of fish, in a pond

fish stocking level—the number of inches of fish that can live in your pond safely without extra filtration

filtration—a general term referring both to mechanical filtration or removal of particulate matter from water and also to bio-filtration, which involves nitrifying bacteria to convert ammonia into nitrite and nitrite into nitrate. (Nitrate is relatively harmless to fish; ammonia and nitrite are toxic to them.)

formal ponds—ponds designed in shapes such as circles, squares, and rectangles and conforming to specific design ideas

groundwater—water that collects below the surface of the ground

informal ponds—ponds designed without strict geometric form

lift—the height, usually in feet, the water rises initially from the pump through a tube or hose to the highest point of re-entry into the system

lined pond—a construction that is lined with a watertight synthetic membrane, such as a rubber liner

mechanical filter—a coarse-grade attachment to a pump, preventing debris from circulating through the pump

pedestals—elevation devices within a pond to bring potted plants to appropriately shallow areas

planting shelves—construction established during the excavation of the pond to provide shallow depths for potted plants

pump—the mechanical means, usually submersed, for recycling pond water through a waterfall, stream, or fountain back into the pond

reservoir pond—the largest pond in a system of ponds and water features, providing water to recycle through various water features without lowering the water level of the reservoir pond significantly

runoff water—water traveling over the surface of the ground

surface-to-air ratio—the amount of surface area of pond water not covered by aquatic plants. Open areas are exposed to air, allowing gas exchanges, i.e., gases such as nitrogen or methane escape from the pond water and oxygen from the air enters the water.

underlay—fabric or material installed between the ground excavation and the synthetic membrane, padding the membrane and protecting it

water clarity—simply, how clear the water is

water quality—the chemical balance of water; this may include such factors as municipally supplied chlorine, ammonia, and nitrites

Fish gathered at your waterfall are telling you they'd like more oxygen.
Photo by H. Nash

a maximum, the more likely you will need filtration to maintain fish-safe water quality. The safest way to begin pondkeeping with fish is to stock your pond lightly, adding more fish later as you become more knowledgeable and comfortable with the garden.

The amount of space you allow for your fish is important for two reasons. The fish load, or density of fish in the water, affects water quality. Fish produce solid wastes and ammonia, both of which affect the water quality and health and lives

If you plan to include koi, be sure your pond is large enough to keep them in good health. Photo by H. Nash

of your fish. By keeping the fish load on the low side of your possible stocking level, you are less likely to encounter these problems.

The other reason for watching the amount of fish in the pond is that fish require adequate oxygen in the water. While your fish need a certain amount of oxygen in the water, to a certain degree, you control that availability. Oxygen enters your pond water primarily at the surface where it contacts the air. If you have much surface coverage by plants, that contact is diminished. Providing aeration by recycling water from a waterfall or fountain can ease oxygen deficiencies. Your fish will often tell you they'd like more oxygen; they congregate around water entry points or gasp and gulp at the surface.

Water Depth

Goldfish and mosquito fish (*Gambuzi*) survive quite happily in typical water garden depths up to two feet. Koi, on the other hand, which grow much larger, require vertical swimming exercise for optimum health. This means at least three feet of depth. Many experts recommend as much as five feet of depth for proper koi keeping.

Water temperature is also impacted by the depth of the pond. A very shallow pond, 18 inches deep for example, heats up much faster and to higher temperatures than one that is two or three feet deep. Likewise, an above-ground pond, which has sides exposed to ambient temperatures, also experiences greater fluctuations in temperature. The typical pond fish—koi and goldfish—are cold-water

fish. Water temperatures of 90°F and above stress these fish and put their health at risk. If you live in a climate where the water temperatures reach such levels, either plan a deeper point within your pond where the water will stay cooler or stock your pond with a breed of fish more tolerant of your climatic conditions.

Water Quality

Contrary to what you might initially think, *water quality* does not refer to *water clarity*. Water clarity, or clear water, is desirable for seeing and enjoying fish. However, toxins such as ammonia, nitrite, and methane and hydrogen sulfide gases, are invisible and may exist in perfectly clear water. Good pond hygiene helps keep these toxins under control, as does maintaining a below-maximum stocking level of

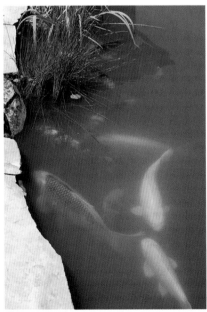

Murky water may still be perfectly safe for your fish. Photo by H. Nash

fish. Bio-filtration that enhances the naturally occurring nitrogen cycle within the pond may also become necessary once your fish have grown and multiplied. (Yes, they breed!)

Adequate dissolved oxygen in the water is part of water quality, too. A sufficient surface-to-air ratio is usually adequate for the lightly stocked pond. Gentle aeration where a waterfall enters enhances that level. Remember, warm water holds less oxygen than cooler water. If your climate presents days of extremely hot weather (90°F and above), plan for 2- to 3-foot- or even 3- to 4-foot-deep areas in the pond to maintain cooler, oxygen-saturated water for your fish.

Ponds for Plants

Do you picture your backyard pond as a Monet vision of sparkling water graced with confections of water lilies? Aquatic plants are the heart and soul of a water garden. If you know ahead of time what plants you wish to grow, you can plan your pond for optimum conditions. And, unlike plants you put in a garden in the soil—these plants don't have to be watered!

Space

One of the real joys of aquatic plants is that there are so many of them! Some plants are suited to the very large pond, such as Mexican papyrus, which grows over 10 feet tall, and water lilies with leaves a foot in diameter and blossoms 10 inches across. There

Large and very tall plants are in proportion for the larger pond.
Photo by H. Nash

are plants of diminutive size suited to the smallest ponds—micro-cattails that grow only 12 to 18 inches tall and dwarf and pygmy water lilies with leaves only 2 or 3 inches across and blooms the size of a quarter. Whatever plants you grow

in your pond, most will be potted in their own containers. While this gives you some control over their space requirements, the vigorous, healthy growth of each plant requires consideration of its mature habit. Unless you are an avid water lily collector filling the pond to the brim with lilies, plan for serene reflections of your plants in the water, to allow the air-to-surface gas exchanges so important to your fish.

Water Depth

If you recall where you've seen aquatic plants in nature, you'll remember that they grow around the shallow edges of water. Marginal aquatic plants like cattail, arrowhead, water iris, and sweet flag all grow in saturated soils and in up to 2–6 inches of water. Water lilies, too, grow in relatively shallow water—usually from 12 to 24 inches in depth, and occasionally in up to 36 inches. What does this mean to your water garden plans? You must either provide pedestals to prop up plants to their optimum depths or provide different depths within your construction for the plants.

Select shorter and smaller plants for the small to tub-sized garden. Shown is the hardy pygmy water lily N. tetragona.
Photo by Michael Duff

Observe how aquatic plants grow in the wild to plan for them within your pond.
Photo by H. Nash

DESIGN YOUR POND TO FIT YOUR LANDSCAPE

A water garden is not set in the middle of your driveway, surrounded by asphalt. To create the greatest sense of beauty and tranquility, it is nestled into your landscape. Ideally, you already have a perfect spot for your pond, but you can re-create the terrain of your yard to suit your envisioned garden. As long as the pond design agrees with your home and yard design, it will enhance the experience of your private haven.

Geometrical shapes define the more formal pond. Photo by Richard Sacher

TYPES OF AQUATIC PLANTS

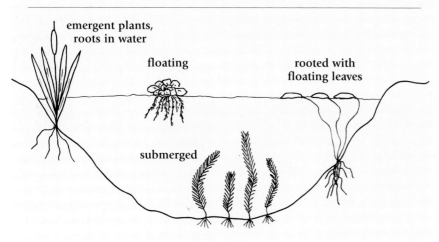

emergent plants, roots in water

floating

rooted with floating leaves

submerged

The Formal Pond

Generally, shapes such as squares, circles, and rectangles befit formal pond designs. Set within a landscape of formally delineated lines and areas, geometrically designed ponds can take the form of reflecting pools highlighted by a fountain or the shimmer of fish, or they can be graced with reflecting circles of water lily plants.

Most backyards are best suited by informally designed ponds.   Photo by H. Nash

The Informal Pond

Set off a deck, among flower beds, or along a garden path, the informally designed pond suits most landscapes and home designs and offers the most creative latitude.

Where to Site the Pond?

Consider Sun Exposure

Ideally, a water garden rife with flowering aquatic plants does best in a very sunny location. But what if your yard doesn't offer such a site? Several types of water lily will bloom in only 3 to 4 hours of sunlight, and most will fare nicely with only 6 hours daily. Even a shady pond has plant options, although not as colorful as those offered by the sunny pond. Check the plant lists on page 124 for plants suited to less-than-sunny locations.

Dubbed the "rainforest" pond, this shady setting is lush with plantings both inside and outside the pond.   Photo by H. Nash

Consider Drainage

Your natural impulse to site the pond in that wet spot in the yard is best not pursued. Groundwater can force a liner up out of the pond, and a runoff collection point in the yard invites chemically treated waters into the pond—a risk to both plants and fish. Check your water table, if only by digging a hole to your proposed pond's depth and allowing it to stand open through your wettest season. Does water collect and stand in the bottom of the hole? If it does, install perimeter drainage to direct the groundwater away from the site. If surface water runs into the area, a camouflaged drainage ditch can redirect water away from the pond. By constructing the pond edges slightly above the surrounding elevation with the inner edges tilted slightly upwards, you can also discourage runoff from entering the pond.

That standing pool of water in your yard is not the best site for your new pond!
Photo by H. Nash

Consider Enjoyment

Site your pond where you can enjoy it most. If you spend much time outside on your deck or patio, nearby is the logical choice. Consider also the delight of viewing the pond from inside the house. It's amazing how relaxing it is to glimpse the pond as you pass a window inside. However, if young children in the family or in the neighborhood are a concern, site the pond where it can be enjoyed the most while still posing the fewest security problems.

Consider Zoning Regulations

Before you proceed with your pond plans, check that your community allows you to install one! Sometimes, zoning ordinances specify that a body of water deeper than 18 inches deep must have a fence around it. Also, consider insurance liability. Check with both your community authorities and your insurance carrier. It is entirely possible to have a lovely water gar-

If digging a hole in your yard is not an option, tub gardens offer great variety. Photo by Bob Romar and courtesy of Maryland Aquatic Nurseries

The shallow stream garden offers a way to enjoy water in the garden without digging a hole. Photo by H. Nash

den only 18 inches deep, and to winter it successfully in colder climates. Some subdivisions and homeowners' associations have such stringent regulations that swimming pools and ponds of any type are not allowed. If this is the case in your area, you can populate your yard with tub and container gardens. Stream gardens (serviced by hidden reservoirs) may be another alternative.

Plan for Safety

Children

The most obvious way to keep children safe around a pond is to install it in a fenced area that prevents their access. In addition, you may wish to consider adding closely spaced rail-

ings on bridges or decks that invite pondside observation.

Constructing the pond with the edges elevated above ground level to 12 inches or more is another way to help prevent accidents.

Likewise, constructing wide planting shelves around the inner perimeter of the pond can prevent disasters. Planting shelves for marginal aquatics are usually only 12 inches deep. By making such a shelf wide enough to support a person's body, as much as 24-36 inches wide, a spill into the pond need be nothing more than a mere dousing with an easy exit. Such shelves offer yet another safety service: they provide "steps" for safe and easy entry and exit from the pond. Since pond liners are slippery when wet, a sloped side can be treacherous.

As yet another precaution, plan to have secure edges around the pond. Rocks that are simply laid in place may tip when stepped on. Stones used around the edge of a pond must be large enough and substantial enough that an adult can step on an edge and the rock

Constructing a very wide, shallow shelf around the perimeter of your pond provides a safety net in case of accidental tumbles. Photo by Oliver Jackson

will remain firmly in place. Mortar rocks into place for stability and then regularly monitor them for steadfastness.

Electricity

Electricity and water do not mix. Running a pump to recycle the water through a waterfall, fountain, or filter requires a safe electrical source. Electrical outlets should be waterproof and should be no closer than four feet from the pond. Conduits should be safely buried by a professional electrician or checked by a professional for proper installation. Electrical cords, even outdoor grade, are dangerous left lying on the ground!

Electrical outlets should have protective covers, ground-fault interrupters, and low voltage. Photo by Oliver Jackson

PLAN YOUR BUDGET

Start out by planning your dream pond. Compute the cost of installing everything you desire. Consider if the project can be constructed in stages—for example, the reservoir or largest pond, the first year; a stream, the second; and another pond in the third. Planning the largest pond first allows you to add features later

that recycle water from that source. Starting with the smaller pond at the top of the stream, for example, might limit the capability of your stream addition because it might not be possible to accommodate the water required to run the next addition. Don't forget to include the cost of extras, such as for landscaping and such structures as a bridge, a deck, or a gazebo.

Computing Materials Needed

The easiest construction for the do-it-yourselfer is the lined pond. Price the various liners available. Laminated plastics and PVC are less expensive than the thicker synthetic rubber EPDM. Check the guarantees and warranties on the liners you would consider. If you wish the pond to last for many years, you'll want to go with the thickest and strongest you can find. Don't forget, when you think about sturdy liner material, to ask yourself, will my pets or will neighborhood dogs take a swim—they have toenails! Surprisingly, rocks may be the most expensive item on your list.

Liner Computation

Unless you go with a precut liner, wait until you've dug the actual excavation before purchasing your liner. This allows you to purchase based on exact measurements. (Although glues and adhesive tapes are available for attaching liner pieces, they may develop leaks in time.) Figure your liner size by adding double the depth to *both* the length and width of the broadest points of the pond. Add another

Although you may plan to end up with a double pond, you can always build the project in stages, one feature at a time. Photo by H. Nash

foot to each dimension because you will tuck in the liner around the edges. Multiply these total amounts by each other to give you the square footage of liner required. Figure the liner needs for waterfalls and streams the same way; however, you can overlap pieces from higher areas into lower ones.

Underlay

To protect the liner from rocks or roots, supply an underlay for the full liner. Special fabric can be purchased for this. You can also use discarded carpet or layers of newspaper or cardboard. Providing 2 or 3 inches of sand is another padding often recommended for the bottom of the excavation. Sand is sold by the ton. One ton equals approximately 20 cubic feet. If you have many tree roots, consider using a special landscape fabric treated to repel root growth.

FORMULAE

Length + 2 × depth + one foot × Width + 2 × depth + one foot = square feet of liner needed

Formulae for computing gallons of water in your pond:

Length × width × depth × 7.48 = gallons per cubic foot for a natural pond

2 × 3.14 × depth × 7.48 = gallons per cubic foot for a round pond

Select rocks for your project that fit naturally into the scheme of your yard.
Photo by H. Nash

Rocks

As you consider what type of rock to put around the edge of your pond, coordinate the design with your home and landscape, and don't forget to consider the weight and cost of your possible selections.

❧ Featherock weighs approximately 64 pounds per cubic foot and is the lightest weight of large rocks. These rocks, available in blacks, browns, and reds, are quite porous and abrasive. Handle them only with gloves on and do not use them where people might come into contact with them. Featherock can be carved for plumbing and waterfall-type structures.

❧ Granite weighs approximately 200 pounds per cubic foot. To lift, move, and place even a small granite rock may require more than one person. Large granite rocks require mechanical assistance, along with site accessibility by the machinery.

❧ Marble weighs approximately 150 pounds per cubic foot, which makes it nearly as difficult to manage. Also, marble can alter the water chemistry by making the water soft.

❧ Commonly used flagstone-type rocks are in the granite-weight range. In 2- to 4-inch thicknesses, they can be managed by one to two people. Rock and stone centers are accustomed to dealing with pondbuilders who show up to hand-select these stones! You'll need to know the perimeter measurement of your pond edge to select enough stone. (The stone, however, will be sold by the ton and will be weighed after your selection.) Generally, count on one ton of stone to cover 70–100 square feet.

❧ Cobbles, usually of a size to fit in two open hands, may be selected for lining a stream bed or for embedding into mortar as a full cover on the pond liner. They are sold 30 to 35 to a ton.

❧ Bricks, new or used, are figured at 4.5 bricks per square foot, laid flat.

Mortar

You may need mortar for setting the rock edging of your pond or for embedding cobbled river rock on top of the pond liner. Determine where you might need mortar in your construction and figure on a 2-inch thickness for the area. Mortar is sold by the 80-pound bag, premixed, to cover a 4-square-foot area at a 2-inch thickness.

Miscellaneous Finishing Supplies

If your pond design calls for low maintenance treatments around it, consider:

⋙ Ground cover aggregates and pea gravel are sold by the ton. A depth of 2 inches requires 100 square feet of stone.

⋙ Stone bark and crater rock give approximately 225 square feet of 2-inch-deep coverage per ton.

⋙ Shredded bark mulch is sold by the yard. One yard covers 100 square feet at a 3-inch depth.

⋙ Pulverized topsoil is also sold by the yard or the ton. One yard equals approximately one ton. One ton/yard equals 27 cubic feet.

Professional Help

If you have plenty of time, a strong back, and muscles, the only help you may need to hire may be the electrician. We know of one pond owner who spent an entire summer digging out a large pond. Thoroughly happy with his pond, he now comments, "I lost 45 pounds but wouldn't recommend it as a weight-loss program!" Most backyard ponds can be dug out, the liner set, and the edge constructed by you and a friend or two. If your yard is accessible, you may wish to consider having a backhoe come in for the roughing-out of the excavation, especially if you plan a pond of any size. Our 100 × 50-foot and 3-foot-deep, shelved and lined pond was dug out by a small bulldozer.

Before you hire someone to work on your pond, check references and observe the person's work. (Your local Better Business Bureau keeps a record of companies with complaints against them, too.) Having access to equipment does not ensure skill in using it for your pond purposes. Arm yourself with information rather than trusting the builder to know it all. The expert who constructs subdivision drainage ponds or your lawn-maintenance people may not know how to build water gardens. You may be asked to make a deposit on the work, but do not complete payment until its completion is satisfactory. It is prudent to have a contract that includes a release from liability for accidents on the job site.

Other Materials

If you will recycle water through your pond—whether through a filter, waterfall, stream, or fountain—you'll need a pump. In many cases, it will be a submersible water garden pump, although for larger ponds, an external pump is often more economical to run and equip for filtration. Pump size is calculated based on the number of gallons per hour it pumps at a one-foot lift, or rise. Pump manufacturers supply charts to indicate how much water flow occurs with any one pump at various lifts. Consider where the pump will sit and how high it must lift the water to determine the lift amount you need. If applicable, add one foot of lift for every 10 feet of tubing or hosing from the pump to the point of water re-entry into the system. See Pump Sizes, in Chapter Six, for more information on how to deter-

If you plan to include many fish or special fish like koi, plan to include a proper filtration system. Photo by H. Nash

mine the proper size pump for your project.

Although pumps are usually equipped with a small mechanical filter to prevent debris from cycling through, you may decide to add further filtration. Many manufactured filters are available, or you can build your own. Filtration needs are determined primarily by your fish stocking level. Even though you may start out with a low fish load, it is wise to plan your initial pond construction so bio-filtration can be added later, if necessary. (See Filtration, Chapter Six.)

Ideas...Where to Put the Pond

Carve out your pond at your front entryway. Photo by H. Nash

Tuck a pond in a corner...
Photo by John Nagle

...or up against your house.
Photo by H. Nash

In the middle of your yard within a landscaped island.
Photo by H. Nash

Create a raised-edge pond within a landscape bed.   Photo by H. Nash

Raised bed gardens are not just for terrestrial plants.   Photo by H. Nash

Build walkways and bridges around your sloped yard...
Photo by H. Nash

...varying your stream width from wide
to a trickle...   Photo by H. Nash

...or tumble a stream down a steep-
sloped yard.   Photo by H. Nash

Tuck a series of raised bed ponds in among your traditional flower beds.
Photo by H. Nash

Make the pond the focal point of a raised landscape bed.   Photo by H. Nash

Just off your deck may be the perfect spot for a small pond.   Photo by Ron Everhart

CHAPTER TWO

Excavation &
Installation

꒜

Learning the Language

bubble level—a carpenter's level

carpenter's level—a straight-edged construction level containing one to three fluid-filled "bubbles" that reflect even level by aligning the level of the fluid

concrete collar—a leveled edge construction of concrete that supplies a stable edge to the feature

excavation—a hole dug into the ground to contain the pond or stream

level—establishing a level pond means that the *upper* edges of the feature allow water to appear evenly settled within its structure. Regardless of the water feature's edge, water sits evenly with relation to the earth

membrane—watertight liner material

poly foam—a synthetic spray used behind waterfall stones to prevent water loss in the system

reservoir pond—the source of recycled water through a waterfall/stream system

shelf/shelve—the form created or the act of creating a shallow level within the formed excavation to site

aquatic plants optimally and/or create access to the pond

spoil—dirt removed from a pond excavation

straight edge—a straight piece of lumber that is used to reach from one level stake to another on which to place a carpenter's level to determine level from one point to another

string level—a string with a bubble weight suspended from it to determine a level construction

tamp—to compact soil, to minimize the effects of settling and the disruption of established levels, and to prevent constructed forms from deterioration and collapse

transit level—a surveyor's tool to determine ground levels using a transit beam and a marked measuring stick

underlay—a layer of protective material beneath the pond liner membrane to minimize the likelihood of puncture from surfacing rocks, roots, etc.

weir—the edge of a rock over which water flows in a waterfall construction

LEVELING THE POND

How well I remember our first pond construction. We tried not to cut any grass. We hired a fellow to dig out the backyard for the pond. I romped around the excavation holding the transit, proudly announcing the level achieved. Later, when we filled the pond, one side was a full foot higher than the other! Oh, we had leveled the *bottom* of the pond. We learned the hard way that water seeks its own level—it doesn't matter how level the bottom is; the *upper edge* determines whether the water *looks* level. I spent an entire summer establishing a true level for the edges of that pond. Even if the pond you build is smaller than our first one of 50 × 100 feet, the principles remain the same—*the upper edges must be level to avoid a lopsided appearance.*

Transit Levels

These systems require a person to stand at each point while another person sights through a transit. Easy to operate, the equipment can be rented.

Line Levels

This system involves the use of short stakes pounded into the ground. Pieces of string are strung tautly from stake to stake, and a level is hung from connecting string to establish the level.

The laser level is an adaptation of the transit level and requires only one person.
Photo by H. Nash

Carpenter's Level/ Bubble Levels

Probably the level most easily used by the individual homeowner is the carpenter's or bubble level. This level is available from local hardware stores in both short and long forms. Pound stakes into the ground close enough to set the level across two stakes. Using a longer level decreases the number of stakes necessary. A measurement on a base stake establishes the level for all further measurements, with each stake measured to be level with the preceding stake. Once the perimeter stakes are level, use a straight board (a long, level plank laid across the pond from stake to stake) to ascertain the level across the pond.

Stake one end of the string at the desired level. Pull the string tightly and adjust its height until the bubble is centered in the level. Photos by Eamonn Hughes

A small carpenter's spirit level determines levels from side to side of a narrow stream excavation.   Photo by H. Nash

Water Level

A clear tube attachment or clear hose, used in conjunction with level-marked stakes, reflects the level point of the water within the tube.

By attaching clear hosing to the end of a garden hose, you can determine levels across larger excavations.
Photo by Eamonn Hughes

EXCAVATION

Before you begin to dig, mark the outline of your pond. Establish the levels of the pond's upper edges. If you must add soil to one side of the pond, be sure to tamp the added soil to lessen any settling. Ideally, you should wait a season for the ground to settle—but who wants to wait? Tamp it well! (And leave enough extra liner around the edges to accommodate possible settling.)

If you're digging the pond out of existing turf, remove the grass sod in squares of manageable size and save them for use around the pond or elsewhere. Dig your first level to a depth for your pond edging stonework. (To avoid runoff water from entering the pond, be sure to provide for a slightly elevated siting for the pond edging.)

Dig out the area a layer at a time. This allows you to provide for any shelving. Keep a tarp next to the excavation to prevent the spoil from killing the grass. Keep your topsoil separate from the lower, infertile soil. Use this good soil in planting beds around your new pond or transfer it to other planting beds. As you hit the levels desired, mark the edges of the shelves. Carving the shelves with the outer edge at a slight tilt upward from the pond side forestalls degradation of the shelf edge and ensures that potted plants remain stable on the shelf.

Make the bottom level approximately two inches lower than the desired depth of the pond to accommodate a layer of sand beneath the liner. Slope the bottom to one deepest point or to an actual sump hole. Make this area wide enough to hold your pump. This will make any future draining easier. (Otherwise you will have to sop up water with towels!) Note that this lowest level may not be where you will operate the pump, but it will facilitate drainage and cleaning.

Preformed ponds are available in a variety of sizes and shapes. Photo by H. Nash

Waterfall and stream courseways are also available in preformed units.
Photo by Oliver Jackson

PREFORMED POND INSTALLATION

Establish the levels of the ground where you will install your preformed pond. Turn the preformed unit upside down and set it on the ground where you will install it. Mark the outline with chalk, cat lit-

ter, or spray paint. Excavate as above, matching the depth of any shelf. If you dig exactly to the depth of the pond shell, adding two inches of sand in the bottom will elevate the upper edges slightly above ground level to avoid surface runoff from entering. Excavate an extra several inches around the outside diameter for backfilling with soil and sand to prevent ground heaving in cold weather, if ground heaving occurs in your climate.

Once the pond is set within the excavation, check that the upper edges are level. Fill the pond with water and simultaneously fill around the outside with shovels of sand watered in with a slowly drizzling hose. If the pond level is slightly off, jiggle the pond form in its sand setting to make it level.

INSTALLING A LINED POND

Mark the outline of your excavation on the ground with chalk, cat litter, or spray paint. Pound in stakes close enough to allow the use of the carpenter's level from stake to stake. Use a level piece of wood (a straight edge) to reach across the width and length of the excavation to verify level. (You can also use a stake set in the center of the pond excavation to check the level from the center to each perimeter stake.) Check the level as you work!

Excavate a shovel's-depth trench around the outline of your pond. Next, excavate the first layer across the entire excavation. Save any grass sod in a shady place for future use. Excavate to the first shelf layer, one shovel's depth at a

time, while piling the topsoil on to a nearby tarp or hauling it away by wheelbarrow. Once you have reached the depth of any shelves you plan to include, mark their outline. Be sure the shelves will be wide enough to support plants and act as stairsteps. Also, if you reinforce the edges of the pond with concrete blocks or other means, make the shelves that much wider.

Once you have reached the bottom depth, slope the excavation to one lowest point to allow future drainage. If you plan to supply a bottom drain to the pond, as is often recommended for koi ponds, you will need to use a trencher. Be sure that any drains have wide enough diameters, matching the drain to be installed into the liner, and that there are no elbow curves that might clog. Direct your drainage to a hidden cistern or suitable drainage site. Kits are available for intrusion through the liner. Follow the manufacturer's directions for installation.

Install any upper edge reinforcement, checking level carefully.

Add two inches of sand to the entire bottom excavation. Cover this with underlay or a thick layer of newspaper, cardboard, or old carpeting. If you use carpeting with rubber backing, slash through it in several places so groundwater will not collect between it and the liner and float your liner. Hold newspapers in place by spraying them lightly with a hose.

Lay out your liner to warm in the sun. If the day is very warm, you may need to use gloves to handle the liner, as it will absorb heat.

An underlay of special fabric, carpeting, or newspaper will protect the pond liner from rocks that work up through the ground.
Photo by Oliver Jackson

Center it in the excavation to ensure that a foot overlaps all the way around. Fit the liner to the excavation, working from the bottom up and consolidating folds into fewer numbers, folding away from the primary line of sight. Use bricks or stones to hold the liner edges in place, adjusting as necessary to avoid stretching the liner as the pond fills.

Begin filling the pond with water, adjusting the liner from the bottom up to a proper fitting. Check your upper edge levels again as the water approaches them. Once you are certain the water is level within the pond, drain enough water to allow comfortable working areas around the edge.

Waterfalls and streams whose liners overlap the main pond liner should be installed before the edge of the pond is finished.

INSTALLING A LINER POND WITH A CONCRETE COLLAR

Sandy soils, non-compacted soil, and any soil that freezes in the winter present special problems of maintaining a top-level edge to your pond over time. A concrete collar may be the answer.

After removing the sod from the pond area, mark the outline of your pond on the ground. (Removing it in manageable strips allows you to store it in a shady location for use elsewhere.) Pound in pointed stakes 12 to 18 inches away from your outline mark and level them with your carpenter's level. Double-check the level in reverse direction and across the pond's span. Excavate a trench six inches deep around the outline of your pond. Your trench should be dug close enough to your level-stakes to be sure the edge will be level.

If you plan a waterfall, you can excavate an area large enough to accommodate the structure. Since this area is likely to be several square feet, strengthen the concrete with mechanic's wire mesh. To do this, lay a 2- to 4-inch layer of concrete and place the mechanic's wire on it. Then cover the remaining 2 to 4 inches with concrete to bring it level with the surrounding collar.

Fill in the trench dug for your collar with ready-mix concrete, smoothing the top and verifying that it is perfectly level with the staked measurements. (If you are pouring concrete on a hot day, be sure to spray it with water throughout the day to keep it from curing and setting too quickly.) Once the collar has set firmly enough to walk on, you can begin excavating the interior of the pond.

Mark your pond outline on the ground and measure its level.   Photo by Dave Artz

Dig a shallow trench around the outer perimeter of your projected pond and use the earth around it as your form for the poured concrete. Check that the concrete is level as you proceed. Create a concrete pad, reinforced if necessary, for your waterfall area.   Photo by Dave Artz

Other Ways to Help Attain a Level Top Edge for Your Pond

1. Another way to establish a solid and level top edge to your pond is with concrete builder's blocks. Remove any sod from the area and mark the level of your planned excavation with stakes. Dig a trench wide enough to accommodate the blocks. As you set them within the trench, be sure they align level with your stakes. Excavate the interior portion of your pond.

Concrete blocks can form a stable edge for your pond.   Photo by Oliver Jackson

2. Use a professional grade of landscape edging for your pond edge. The advantage of this method is that you can bring your pond liner up over the top of the narrow edging and dip it back down behind the edging. This allows you to bring turf up to the edge of the pond. Again, mark the level of the excavation area. Excavate a trench to a depth to accommodate the landscape edging. Pound in the metal stakes at the outer edge so

Special edging forms or professional landscape edging can form the upper edge of your pond.   Photo courtesy of Charleston Aquatic Nursery

The landscape edging is secured by stakes in the ground and its level carefully verified. The liner fits crisply over the thin ridge to allow turf or surrounds brought up to the pond's edge.   Photo courtesy of Charleston Aquatic Nursery

they are level and attach the landscape edging all around. This works best if you have a shelf constructed around the perimeter of the entire pond.

SHELVING CONSIDERATIONS

Excavating your pond in various levels provides ready-made areas for different potted aquatic plants. Marginal aquatics, for example, typically grow with only one to four inches of water over the top of the pot. A shelf area only 12 inches from the top of the pond is a handy place to set these edge plants. A shelf area two feet deep provides ready-made areas for most water lilies. Shelf areas that descend progressively by a foot each to the pond bottom create handy steps for the pondkeeper who might need to enter the pond to work. Even a two-foot-deep pond benefits from built-in steps. (18-inch depths are navigable, if awkward.)

A wet liner is slippery. If the pond sides are sloped, entry and exit can be treacherous for the gardener! However, in areas where raccoons are a problem, creating these shallow shelf areas is an open invitation to predators.

If you create shelves in your excavation, make them wide enough! Over time the soil behind your pond can deteriorate and round off any edge excavation. (If your soil is sandy, you may wish to reinforce even your shelves as you did the top edge. A wooden frame over the entire excavation may prove advisable in sugar-sand conditions.) A shelf less than a foot wide allows for only one pot's width of plants. Wider shelves allow for attractive groupings of potted plants; they also provide an important safety feature: a child who tumbles into the pond has enough room not to fall into even deeper water.

No, you do not *have* to construct shelving areas in your pond. Plants requiring shallow depths can be propped up on pedestals such as plastic milk crates, plastic-coated shelf units, or even aged bricks and

Placing a stepping stone on the plant shelf creates a fish-feeding area in your pond.
Photo by Oliver Jackson

concrete blocks. If you use concrete blocks, however, seal them with protective paint to prevent the lime from leaching into your pond water. Blocks can also be rinsed well many times to keep them from affecting the pH of the water.

WATERFALL AND STREAM INSTALLATIONS

Waterfalls are desirable amendments to pond construction for several reasons: they are beautiful to look at, they sound good, and they provide a way of recycling the water for aeration and filtration. Waterfalls do not have to be hillside features, they can be kept in proportion to the pond. (A six-foot waterfall would look unnatural with a 2 × 3 foot pond!) For our purposes, streams are an adaptation of the waterfall.

You do not need a natural hillside for a waterfall or a stream. The dirt excavated for your pond can be put to use to create the elevation necessary for a waterfall or stream. Keep the mound of soil in proportion to the reservoir pond and the natural terrain. Don't pile the dirt in one spot and declare it your waterfall. Blend it into the surrounding terrain to naturalize your construction. A waterfall only a foot wide, for example, may be set within a mound that is 6 feet wide or more. Use the remainder of the mound for rock placements and backdrop plantings.

To recycle water through a waterfall or a stream/waterfall, the bottom pond that is the source of the recycling water is called the reservoir pond. For a small fall only a foot high at the pond edge, you won't have to worry much about the volume of water in use in the waterfall system. More expansive designs, however, must take into consideration the amount of water drawn out of the reservoir pond and put into use in the system above. See the chart on page 34 for computing the necessary size of a reservoir pond to service various waterfall/stream systems.

Regardless of the size of your waterfall/stream, it must be lined to prevent water loss into the surrounding terrain. Likewise, the sides of the water channel must be high enough to prevent splash loss. There will be evaporative loss in a waterfall/stream system, but not as much as with a fountain that exposes the water fully to the air. In dry periods, you may need to "top off" the system once every week or two.

It is not necessary to use a single piece of liner for both the reservoir pond and the waterfall/stream. Actually, using a single piece can be quite awkward to work with in construction. A separate piece of liner can be used for each level of the waterfall/stream construction. Simply overlap the upper level liner over the next level liner by several inches. Rockwork camouflages the overlap area and holds the flap back against the structure. Bring your liner up the sides of the water channel at least 4 inches. Tuck the liner back into the soil or hide it with rocks.

Create a small stream and waterfall in the spoil from your pond excavation.
Photo by H. Nash

Computing Reservoir Pond Size Required for Waterfall/Stream

Water Drops in Reservoir Pond with Stream System
Note: Assume 3-inch depth of water in stream courseway and 3-foot width of stream.
Drops in inches when stream is designated by feet in length:

Reservoir Pond in feet	10'	15'	20'	25'	30'	40'	50'	75'	100'
4 x 4	3.9	5.6	7.8	9.8	11.7	15.63	19.53	29	39.06
4 x 5	3.13	4.69	6.25	7.8	9.38	12.5	15.63	23.44	37.5
4 x 6	2.6	3.9	5.21	6.5	7.8	10.42	13.02	19.532	6.04
4 x 7	2.23	3.35	4.46	5.6	6.7	8.93	11.16	16.74	22.32
4 x 8	1.95	2.93	3.9	4.89	5.90	7.81	9.77	14.65	22.06
5 x 5	2.5	3.75	5	6.25	7.5	10	12.5	18.75	30
5 x 6	2.08	3.13	4.17	5.2	6.25	8.33	10.42	15;.63	20.83
5 x 7	1.79	2.68	3.55	4.46	5.35	7.14	8.93	13.39	17.86
5 x 8	1.56	2.34	3.13	3.9	4.7	6.25	7.81	11.72	15.63
5 x 9	1.39	2.08	2.78	3.47	4.17	5.56	6.94	10.42	13.89
5 x 10	1.25	1.88	2.5	3.12	3.75	5	6.25	9.38	12.5
6 x 6	1.74	2.6	3.46	4.3	5.2	6.94	8.68	13.02	17.36
6 x 7	1.49	2.23	2.98	3.72	4.5	5.95	7.44	11.16	14.89
6 x 8	1.3	1.95	2.6	3.3	3.9	5.21	6.51	9.77	13.02
6 x 9	1.16	1.74	2.3	2.9	3.5	4.63	5.79	8.68	11.57
6 x 10	1.04	1.56	2.08	2.6	3.1	4.12	5.21	7.81	10.42
7 x 7	1.28	1.91	2.55	3.18	3.8	5.1	6.38	9.57	12.76
7 x 8	1.12	1.67	2.23	2.79	3.35	4.46	5.58	8.37	11.16
7 x 9	.99	1.49	1.98	2.48	2.97	3.97	4.96	7.44	9.92
7 x 10	.89	1.34	1.79	2.23	2.67	3.57	4.46	6.7	8.93
7 x 12	.74	1.12	1.49	1.86	2.23	2.98	3.73	5.58	7.44
7 x 14	.64	.96	1.28	1.59	1.91	2.55	3.19	4.78	6.38
8 x 8	.98	1.46	1.95	2.44	2.9	3.9	4.89	7.32	9.77
8 x 10	.78	1.17	1.56	1.95	2.34	3.13	3.91	5.86	7.81
8 x 12	.65	.98	1.3	1.63	1.95	2.6	3.26	4.88	6.51
8 x 14	.56	.84	1.12	1.39	1.67	2.23	2.79	4.19	5.58
8 x 16	.49	.73	.98	1.22	1.46	1.95	2.44	3.3	4.88
9 x 10	.69	1.04	1.39	1.74	2.08	2.78	3.47	5.21	6.94
9 x 12	.58	.87	1.16	1.45	1.74	2.31	2.89	4.34	5.79
9 x 14	.496	.74	.99	1.24	1.48	1.98	2.48	3.72	4.96
9 x 16	.43	.65	.87	1.09	1.17	1.74	2.17	3.26	4.34
9 x 18	.39	.58	.77	.96	1.16	1.54	1.93	2.89	3.86
10 x 10	.63	.94	1.25	1.56	1.88	2.5	3.13	4.69	6.25
10 x 12	.52	.78	1.04	1.3	1.56	2.08	2.6	3.9	5.36
10 x 14	.45	.67	.89	1.12	1.34	1.92	2.23	3.35	4.46
10 x 16	.39	.59	.78	.98	1.17	1.56	1.95	2.93	3.9
10 x 18	.35	.52	.69	.87	1.04	1.39	1.74	2.6	3.47
10 x 20	.31	.47	.63	.78	.94	1.25	1.56	2.34	3.13
12 x 15	.35	.52	.69	.87	1.04	1.39	1.74	2.6	3.47
12 x 24	.22	.33	.43	.54	.65	.87	1.04	1.65	2.17
15 x 20	.21	.31	.42	.52	.63	.83	1.04	1.56	2.08
15 x 25	.17	.23	.33	.42	.5	.67	.83	1.25	1.67
15 x 30	.14	.19	.28	.35	.42	.56	.69	1.04	1.39
20 x 25	.13	.17	.25	.31	.38	.45	.63	.94	1.25
20 x 30	.10	.14	.21	.26	.31	.42	.52	.78	1.04
20 x 40	.08	.11	.16	.195	.23	.31	.39	.59	.78

Basic Waterfall/ Stream Construction

Line your water channel with a scrap piece of pond liner membrane. Stack your rocks onto the liner, bringing the edges of the liner up the sides of the channel high enough to prevent water loss. Camouflage the liner with more rocks. Remember that using mortar or concrete as a base of your construction invites leaks at some point, especially in climates where alternating freeze-thaw conditions occur. Liners under the entire structure prevent water loss!

After the concrete has set, remove the form. You are now ready to line your construction.
Photo by Greg Maxwell

A waterfall or stream without much ground-form support can be strengthened with a concrete form. Use the back of your excavation as one wall of your form and use flexible plywood as the inner side.
Photo by Greg Maxwell

Fully line the construction. If you mortar rocks into the lining, be sure to run water long enough that lime no longer shows up in elevated pH readings of the water.
Photo by Greg Maxwell

Hillside waterfalls are constructed much like stairs and are fully lined to prevent water loss. Photo by Eamonn Hughes

Creating a Natural-Looking Stream or Waterfall

1. Once the largest rocks have been set in place on the liner, the sides of the course-way are constructed beginning with a bed of mortar.
Photo by Eamonn Hughes

4. Like a three-dimensional puzzle, rocks are fit together with mortar to create the form of the structure.   Photo by Eamonn Hughes

7. A gentle flow over cobblestones creates pleasing sight and sound.
Photo by H. Nash

2. Set the base rock into the mortar.
Photo by Eamonn Hughes

5. Note as the work proceeds that the liner membrane extends beyond the framework of the structure. It will be tucked into the surrounding soil and hidden by more rocks and plants.   Photo by Eamonn Hughes

Creating Your Own Look

Do you want your water to fall in a clear sheet, or do you want it to tumble over cobbled rocks? To make the water fall in a clear sheet, you'll need a sharp-edged, flat stone as your *weir* (edge of the fall). You'll also need the water to flow with enough force to fall in a clear sheet. An undersized pump may produce only a drizzle over the rock edge and down the waterfall's face. Wet walls can result, too, if the distance between the levels of your waterfall are too far apart. Generally, you should plan on 100 gallons per

3. To build up the mortar behind and upon the base rock, fit another rock into place.
Photo by Eamonn Hughes

6. Before mortaring in spillway rocks, lay them out dry to check for size and appearance.   Photo by Eamonn Hughes

hour for each inch of weir. Do build your waterfall/stream first before buying the pump! Once your structure is completed, you can accurately compute the size of pump required to produce the look you have in mind.

Vary the distance between falls to create different looks. Use a straight-edged weir for one level and cobbles for another. Start your waterfall several feet back from the pond edge and incorporate a stream bed of level sections between the fall drops. Set a rock at the edge of a straight-edged weir to split the water flow. You'll notice this also enforces the flow of water when used back from the fall edge or in the bed of a stream. Your best source for ideas may be in a nearby state park; take along your camera to record scenes you especially like. Study water and how it moves as you envision your own flowing waters.

Before You Build

Test your designs by arranging and rearranging your rocks. If you're not accomplished working with rocks, you may need to try many different arrangements before you're satisfied. Even if you plan to mortar rocks place, set up your design and test its effects by running water from a hose through the system. Plan to make your rock placements appear natural: rocks rarely sit fully on top of the ground. Often they are embedded to varying depths. Your outer edge rocks can then provide planting pockets for specimen plants and small rock garden plants.

When you are satisfied with your construction, take a picture of it or make a drawing and mark your key rocks with chalk numbers to be sure of returning them properly in the final construction. You can also start your construction at the bottom and work your way up, removing rocks a section at a time and replacing them in the final construction.

Building Tips

1. Line it all!

2. Keep it natural—vary the size of rocks used unless your design calls for a more stylized look.

3. Set in your side rocks first; these will be your larger stones.

4. If you mortar your rocks in place, only an inch or two of mortar is needed to set the rocks. Work in small sections, mortaring in the side rocks first and then proceeding across the bed.

5. Always work from the bottom up.

6. If you have any length at all to your structure, provide curves in the courseway. These create the illusion that the channel is longer and give your feature a sense of mystery and surprise.

7. Poly foam, available at hardware stores, can be used to fill in spaces behind and between rocks where water might otherwise escape the main flow. This material dries to a white/yellow color and can be obtrusive. It expands greatly! Keep a stick handy to push it back into where you are spraying. Sand can be tossed on it while it is still wet—which isn't long—or you can press smaller rocks into it to help camouflage its use. Bubbles that harden can be twisted off later. Once water is running through the system, natural algae growth helps hide it, too. Be especially careful

not to have any visible above the water line; you won't be able to hide it without adding more rocks over it.

8. If you use mortar to finish your construction, either scrub down the mortar joints with vinegar water and multiple rinses or run water through the system long enough that the water pH in the reservoir pond tests below 8.5 before you

Many professional pond builders use a waterproof spray poly foam to fill in behind rocks in waterfalls and streams to prevent water loss behind the rocks.
Photo by Bob Romar and courtesy of Maryland Aquatic Nurseries

Poly foam comes in a pressurized can with a narrow tube attachment for easy application.   Photo by Oliver Jackson

add fish to the reservoir pond. (See Chapter Five.)

Stream Installations

The most critical consideration with longer stream construction is having enough water to service the entire system without producing too great a drop in the water level of the reservoir pond. Eamonn Hughes works from a formula that is presented in the chart on page 34 .

Your stream need not be built into a hillside. A meandering "meadow" stream can be set within what appears to be fairly level terrain. You need provide only a minimum of one inch drop in elevation per ten feet to effect a flow from the uppermost elevation to the reservoir source.

When you excavate for your stream bed, be sure the excavation is deep enough to accommodate

A stream garden can be installed in a fairly flat terrain. Photo by H. Nash

You don't even need a pond to have a stream garden. The water can be recycled from a hidden reservoir that creates a child-safe water feature in your garden.
Photo by H. Nash

the thickness of all rocks plus up to three inches of water and at least 2–3 inches above that. Dig the entire channel wide enough throughout to accommodate the widest section of your feature. You then leave yourself the option of creating more narrow sections, and perhaps even small pools off to the side to grow special aquatic plants.

Use a single piece of liner for your entire stream bed, overlapping it by several inches into the reservoir source. If your stream channel has a drop of several inches at some point, however, you can use separate liner pieces for each section and overlap the liner from the higher elevation over the lower one, as you would in a waterfall construction.

Stream Tips

1. Water tends to flow under rocks in a stream bed. You will need a strong enough flow to create the look you want, or you'll want to mortar or polyfoam the lining rocks to the liner.
2. Lining the stream bed with sand often produces stretches of bare

liner with the sand washing to points of obstruction.
3. Rippling stream effects are created by small pebbles just below the water surface.
4. Naturalize the edges of your stream by carrying the rocks and edge plantings out into the surrounding terrain.
5. Streams can be set among and circle around existing trees in your landscape. Use an underlay beneath your stream liner of specially treated landscape cloth that repels tree root invasion.
6. Effects such as decorative wood posts can be set within the stream bed by anchoring them in mortar and building up stone to conceal the mortar base.
7. Many aquatic plants can be grown at the edge of the stream or within the bed itself. Closely monitor the growth of these plants that they do not fill the stream bed with their roots. An accumulation of roots and debris causes water loss. See the appendix for a list of suggested plants.

Wooden accents are embedded in mortar on the lined stream bed.
Photo by Greg Maxwell

After mortaring smooth pebbles over the liner, the look is complete.
Photo by Greg Maxwell

A second pond can serve as a vegetative filter.
Photo by H. Nash

ADDING TO THE FEATURE

The one lament of most pond owners is that they didn't make the pond big enough. The first question these folks ask is whether they can drain the pond and somehow attach another piece of liner to the existing one. While there are double-sided tapes and special adhesives available, these may not be effective for the life of your pond. The most effective of these tapes or glues require professionally applied heat. Hair dryers do not have enough heat for permanent fixing. Especially if the bond occurs at a very low level of the pond, you risk draining your pond unknowingly beneath winter ice or while you are away on vacation. The safest additions to the existing pond are made at upper levels where such leakage will not endanger your pond plants and fish.

Ideally, plan enlargements as separate but linked features. A second pond, for example, can be twice the size of your first and connect by a waterfall in an adjacent construction or by a stream to a nearby location. Remember to have the second pond either at a slightly higher or at a slightly lower elevation to accommodate a flow of water from one to the other. Ben and Kit Knotts of Florida demonstrate, too, that your system of interconnecting ponds can be as extensive as you want—their backyard paradise includes more than 40 ponds connected by a system of flowing streams!

Edging Treatments for Your Pond

The Traditional Necklace...

In the more formal site, such as this front entry pond, a refined rock necklace provides charm.   Photo by H. Nash

Note that in the traditional necklace design the inner edges of the stones tilt slightly upward to discourage surface runoff from entering the pond.
Photo by H. Nash

Bricks...

A mortared single brick edge caps a lined pond. The liner is secured beneath the formal edge.
Photo by Ron Everhart

Pavers...

A variation of pavers is the rich color of terra cotta tiles. Extend the pond-edge pavers to simulate installation within a patio.   Photo by John Nagle

In this non-mortared construction, the liner is brought back up behind the bottom layer of bricks, maintaining the water level at the first row of stones. With the first row at ground level, the second layer prevents surface runoff from entering the pond. Moisture seeps into the filled area to create a bog edging.
Photo by H. Nash

Set at the edge of a traditionally tiled patio, the outer half of this pond's edge uses same-colored tile for a finished look.   Photo by John Nagle

Creating Texture...

Space flat stonework so that gravel or pebbles fill in between them for a variation in texture. Photo by H. Nash

A classic stone necklace is framed by a ring of gravel and then weed-inhibiting mulch.
Photo by H. Nash

Combine a low-maintenance gravel surround with a flat stone edging that staggers into the gravel. Photo by H. Nash

Large Rocks and Cobbles...

Irregularly shaped rocks, carefully stacked, create a natural appearance.
Photo by H. Nash

A fully cobbled pond edge is easily achieved by covering the pond liner with cobbles and extending them up and over the edge. Mortaring the cobbles in place assures stability. Photo by Greg Jones

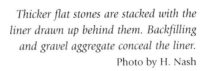

Thicker flat stones are stacked with the liner drawn up behind them. Backfilling and gravel aggregate conceal the liner.
Photo by H. Nash

Large stones require mechanical assistance for placement. Photo by Ron Everhart

Raised Pond Edges...

Plants and Edging...

A concrete-formed raised edge is capped with harmoniously sized capstones mortared in place. Photo by Clifford Tallman

Leave planting pockets in your pond edging for specimen plants. Use plants in scale with your pond size. Photo by H. Nash

Combination Edges...

A pathway between two ponds uses its edging rocks as part of the pond edging. A retaining wall on the opposite side completes this unusual design. Photo by H. Nash

Pendent grasses or daylilies planted near the pond edge soften its perimeter. Photo by H. Nash

CHAPTER THREE

Pond Chemistry

Learning the Language

aerobic bacteria—bacteria that need oxygen to survive

acidic—measuring below neutral pH

alkaline—measuring above neutral pH

ambient temperature—the temperature of the surrounding air

ammonia—a compound of nitrogen and hydrogen, formed in the anaerobic decomposition of organic matter and also added to public water to bond with chlorine to form longer-lived chloramine. NO_3 is fish-toxic, while NO_4 is not.

anaerobic bacteria—bacteria that survive in oxygen-less conditions; often found within soil and facilitating decomposition of organic matter

bio-filtration—the use of media supplied for colonies of nitrifying bacteria to enhance the nitrogen cycle in the pond, to prevent ammonia and nitrite from attaining fish-toxic levels

buffering—the ability of water to resist pH changes following the addition of acid or base

carbonic acid—H_2CO_3, a compound formed by dissolved carbon dioxide and water; an acid added naturally to the pond water by plant respiration, it lowers pH

chlorine—a poisonous gas used to purify water

closed systems—ecological systems that are self-enclosed, without access to surrounding environmental influence

eco-balance—environmental factors balanced in relation to each other to create optimum conditions

natural balance—achieving eco-balance through only natural means

nitrate—the end-product of the nitrogen cycle; generally harmless as found in the garden pond, used by plants as food

nitrogen cycle—a naturally occurring chemical process by which organic wastes produce ammonia which, along with ammonia wastes from fish, converted by bacteria to nitrite, are in turn converted by bacteria into nitrate

nitrobacter bacteria—the aerobic bacteria that convert nitrite into nitrate

nitrosomonas bacteria—the aerobic bacteria that convert ammonia into nitrite

osmoregulatory system—in fish, the system that provides blood to carry oxygen throughout the fish's circulatory system

pH—the concentration of hydrogen ions in water represented logarithmically; a measure of acid in water

photosynthesis—the process by which carbon dioxide and water are transformed in the presence of light and chlorophyll into carbon-containing, energy-rich, organic compounds, with oxygen as a by-product

respiration—the process of obtaining energy from organic material, in effect the opposite of photosynthesis, performed by plants during nighttime hours with the by-product carbon dioxide

water hardness—the concentration of calcium and magnesium salts in the water

zeolite—a soft mineral that absorbs ammonia from water by chemical bonding

The unseen world of water chemistry holds the key to successful pondkeeping.
Photo by Ron Everhart

If you understand basic pond chemistry, you will enjoy your pond much more. Unlike larger natural water features found on country excursions, a small backyard feature is a *closed system*. To establish an eco-balance, so often mentioned in pond literature, you must first understand water chemistry and pond biology within such closed systems. A balanced pond means that both your fish and your plants can co-exist healthfully within the pond. This balance can be achieved naturally or with the use of filtration. To achieve a natural balance, maintain your fish population below the maximum level for your pond. (See Chapter Five.)

CHLORINE AND CHLORAMINE

You need only consider the use of chlorine to determine its potential effect on your pond. A poisonous gas, it is used to purify water and is added to most public water supplies. It can harm both fish and plants, which is why aquarium keepers have jugs of aged water on hand for topping off their indoor fish habitats. Fortunately, chlorine reverts easily to its natural gaseous state and is dissipated from water by spraying the water or by simply letting the water sit for several days.

Many public water suppliers have discovered that the longevity of chlorine can be extended by supplying ammonia to bond with the chlorine to create chloramine. Both chlorine and ammonia are added to the water to effect such bonding. Spraying the water in your pond does not get rid of chloramine, nor does the usual chemical dechlorination treatment. Chloramine's real dangers to your pond are the associated presence of ammonia and the possibility that it will degenerate into ammonia. Ammonia (NO_3) can harm or kill your fish. Often, treated water straight from your tap contains fish-toxic levels of ammonia.

Aquarium chemists and pond supply manufacturers offer products that reduce the chloramine into the fish-safe, nontoxic form of ammonia (NO_4). These products use sodium hydroxymethane sulfinate or di-hydroxymethane to make the non-toxic form of ammonia. Among the most commonly available of these products are Tetra's

Keep your fish population below your pond's maximum stocking level.
Photo by H. Nash

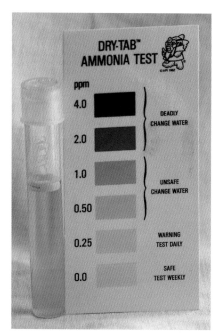

This ammonia test of Indianapolis city water reflects fish-toxic water directly from the tap. Photo by Ron Everhart

AquaSafe NH/CL Formula, Aquarium Pharmaceutical's Ammo Lock2, and Kordon's AmQuel. None of these products remove ammonia from the water; they simply chemically alter the ammonia into a nontoxic form. However, you cannot tell by tests if the toxic form of ammonia has been removed since presently available test kits do not differentiate between the two forms of ammonia. In an established pond, that nontoxic form of ammonia is safely cycled into harmless nitrates. If your water supply is treated with chloramine, any water additions over five percent of the total volume of the pond will require treatment to protect your fish. Treating only the added water is considerably less expensive than treating the entire pond.

If your water supply contains chloramine, using zeolite may be helpful. Zeolite absorbs ammonia, chemically removing it from the water. After the soft, white mineral is saturated with ammonia, it can be "recharged" by submersing it overnight in 5 gallons of water in which is dissolved one pound of non-iodized salt. The ammonia is stripped from the zeolite to form harmless nitrochloric acid and sodium hydroxide, leaving the zeolite free to absorb more ammonia. Commonly available in chip form, zeolite is also available in larger chunks that work well in pond filtration setups.

Even though you keep your fish stocking level below its maximum, bio-filtration units may be advisable if your water contains chloramine. With an established biofilter, you know that harmful ammonia supplied by even minimal water exchanges is safely processed through the nitrogen cycle. (See Chapter Six for information on bio-filters.)

THE NITROGEN CYCLE AND ECO-BALANCE

Whether or not you supply bio-filtration to your pond, and even if you do not have fish in your pond, the nitrogen cycle will occur. Nitrifying and anaerobic bacteria are integral to this cycle. During the decomposition of organic matter in water, ammonia is produced. Ammonia is also produced as fish wastes. Nitrifying bacteria, *Nitrosomonas,* convert ammonia into nitrite, which is then converted by another bacteria, *Nitrobacter,* into nitrate. Ammonia is harmful to fish. Nitrite is even more harmful, as it suppresses a fish's ability to carry oxygen in its bloodstream. Even slight amounts can stress fish. Larger amounts cause them to suffocate. When a pond is first started up or first opened in the spring, measurements of ammonia and nitrite levels indicate where your pond is in this natural cycle. Ammonia peaks first, followed

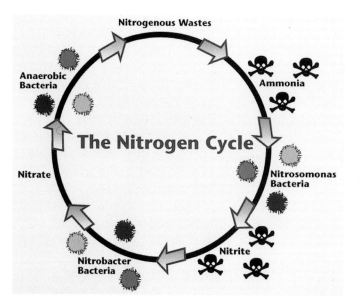

Diagram courtesy of Santa Fe Water Gardens, Santa Fe, New Mexico

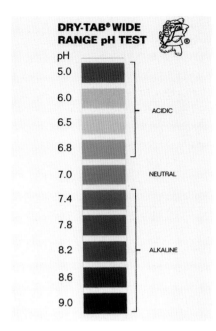

DRY-TAB® WIDE RANGE pH TEST

pH

5.0	
6.0	ACIDIC
6.5	
6.8	
7.0	NEUTRAL
7.4	
7.8	
8.2	ALKALINE
8.6	
9.0	

pH test kits come equipped with a measuring chart, to assess the pH readings of pond water. Protect test tabs from extremes of temperature to preserve their integrity.
Photo by Rich Barker

within a week or so by nitrite. Once the levels of both are negligible, the pond is considered in balance.

Nitrate is usually of no concern to the pondkeeper regarding fish health. However, nitrate is consumed by plants. In the early spring when plants have yet to resume active growth, high levels of nitrate can foster algae blooms or green-water episodes. The oft-heard term "eco-balance" relates to a balanced nitrogen cycle: enough nitrifying bacteria are present to control ammonia and nitrite levels, and enough plants are present to control nitrate levels.

PH AND WATER HARDNESS

In its simplest terms, pH is a measure of acid in water. More precisely, it is the abbreviation for the concentration of hydrogen ions in water. Each pH increment represents a ten-fold difference because the measure is logarithmic. pH readings rise as hydrogen ion concentrations fall, because pH is the negative log of hydrogen concentration. Since each atom of water contains two atoms of hydrogen, these atoms may be exchanged from one molecule to another so that at times free hydrogen atoms are available, just as are molecules with more than 2 atoms of hydrogen or molecules with less than 2 atoms of hydrogen.

With the addition of acidity from plant materials such as sphagnum moss or from rainfall or from chemical additions, pH can be lowered. The most common source of acid in a pond, however, is carbon dioxide produced by plant, animal, and microbial respiration at night. When carbon dioxide dissolves in water, it turns into carbonic acid (H_2CO_3), lowering pH. Hence, testing pond water first thing in the morning will reveal a lowered pH reading, while later in the same day, as oxygen is produced by photosynthesis and carbon dioxide is used, the pH rises. Because the pH fluctuates over a 24-hour period, test the pH at the same time of day for an accurate reading.

Most pond plants and fish are happiest in water within the neutral pH range of around 7.0. Wide swings in pH often occur in green-water ponds and indicate the need to bring the algae-ridden water under control. However, most pond fish are acclimated to these natural swings and are not at risk. If, in the absence of green water, your pH reading varies by more than 1.5 during the 24-hour period, consider buffering the water to avoid stressing the fish. A pH reading of 5.0 can be especially dangerous to fish. Buffering water makes it possible to resist pH changes following the addition of acid or base. Buffered water does not lower its pH too much following the plants' nightly production of carbon dioxide. Chemically, buffers are the product that results after combining a weak acid and a weak base. In aquariums, oyster shell is often used as a buffer. Supplying chemical buffers is expensive and not really necessary unless the water pH is normally below 6.0.

Both goldfish and koi, the most common pond fish, do best in normal to slightly alkaline (between 7 and 8) pH levels. Well water that typically registers as high as 9 is still adaptable by pond fish. Attempting to regulate pH levels may be more dangerous than it is worth. Although your fish can adapt to normally fluctuating levels (that do occur over a period of time), deliberately exposing them to sudden changes in excess of more than 0.2 readings during a 24-hour period can jeopardize them.

Natural remedies are at work in the pond. Alkalinity (the concentration of bases such as calcium carbonate) naturally buffer pH between 7.2 and 8.3. Aeration can drive off excess carbon dioxide produced by plants at night and that would normally result in lower pH. (A good reason not to shut off the waterfall or fountain at night!) Any pH readings that approach dangerous levels in the morning or evening may be best dealt with by doing nothing at all, as these are the peak times.

If your water source pH measures below 6 or above 9.5, you may wish to consult a professional at your local aquarium or pond shop. Do not attempt to alter the pH of the water deliberately by more than 0.2 during a 24-hour period.

Water hardness is often confused with pH, but it is quite different. Water hardness relates to the concentration of calcium and magnesium salts present in your water supply. Both koi and goldfish benefit from hard water, as it reduces the workload of the osmoregulatory system of the fish. For this reason, salt is considered a tonic for weak or stressed fish.

Oxygen and Carbon Dioxide

Oxygen is present in water in a dissolved state. The amount of oxygen dissolving into water is temperature-dependent—as the water temperature increases, the maximum amount of oxygen that will dissolve in it decreases. Conversely, cooler water holds more oxygen. During the summer, when the water temperature approaches the ambient temperature, this can be critical. Fish gulping at the surface or congregating at the entry point

of the water, such as at the waterfall, are a sure sign that the pond water is deficient in oxygen. Although test kits are available to determine oxygen level, they are expensive; fish behavior is a simple, reliable indicator.

How does oxygen enter pond water? The primary source of dissolved oxygen in the pond water is at the surface, where it contacts the surrounding air. The water in ponds heavily stocked with surface plants, such as water lilies, or floating aquatics, such as water hyacinth or duckweed and azolla, may be seriously deprived of oxygen exchange. Watch your fish to see if they are gulping and for surface activity. Supply additional aeration if necessary.

Oxygen also enters water through aeration, either by tumbling into the pond via a waterfall or breaking the surface via a fountain. Spraying the top of an overheated pond with a hose spray provides additional oxygen in an emergency, as does equipping the pond with a long air-stone and air pump. During hot weather, we once had a shipment of floating aquatics arrive that we placed temporarily in a 25-foot diameter koi pond. The fish soon made their distress known, and several died! We removed the bulk of the plants as quickly as possible and used an industrial air compressor to prevent the loss of more of the stressed koi.

Perhaps the greatest danger to your fish comes from submerged aquatic plants mistakenly referred to as "oxygenators." Many people erroneously believe that simply

adding more of these plants will create additional oxygen for their fish. This is certainly true during the daylight hours when sunlight enables photosynthesis to occur in green plants and the by-product is oxygen. However, during the night plants respire. During the process of respiration, plants use oxygen to produce carbon dioxide. This doubly threatens fish: first, the removal of oxygen deprives your fish of it, and secondly, the addition of carbon dioxide to the water lowers the water pH. Both conditions can stress fish. When you have balanced your pond with an appropriate number of submerged aquatic plants, they will add oxygen during the daytime and not deplete it drastically at night. Generally, one to two bunches of these plants per square foot of water surface area is adequate to balance photosynthesis and respiration. If your fish load is too heavy for the pond, your fish will tell you early in the morning that they need more oxygen by gasping at the surface or, worse—by dying for no apparent reason.

While excess carbon dioxide in water can affect the pH, it also reflects a shortage of oxygen. Fortunately, the remedy for increasing oxygen levels, aeration, is the same remedy for ridding the water of excess carbon dioxide. For that reason, it is not necessary to test your water for excess carbon dioxide. If your fish tell you they need more oxygen, listen, and tend to both problems by supplying supplemental aeration to the water.

Ways to Add More Oxygen to Your Pond's Water

A dome fountain adds oxygen to the water while presenting minimal surface agitation and splash that might displease your water lilies. Bubbling geyser-type fountains set at the water surface offer maximum fountain aeration in small ponds.   Photo by Scott Bates

Even a small waterfall offers aeration to the water.   Photo by H. Nash

Although water is aerated upon its return to the pond through this plumbed hand pump, thinning the plants to allow air to touch the water also aids in gas exchanges.
Photo by H. Nash

CHAPTER FOUR

Planting & Tending the Water Garden

Now that your pond is installed and the water is aging, consider the plants you want to grow in it. Many nurseries and books suggest a formula of x amount of each type of aquatic plant to achieve the balance that results in clear, healthy water. However, as had been previously mentioned, pond balance is determined primarily by fish load in the pond. With fish load kept at an appropriate range, a selection of plants can perform other important functions to enhance the desired balance.

Surface floating plants and plants with floating leaves help shade water and discourage the growth of green-water algae. But remember that having a large number of floating-leafed plants in a heavily fish-loaded pond deprives water of oxygen. If your fish exceed your stocking level, provide supplemental aeration to make them more comfortable and cut back on the amount of surface coverage.

Even more important than surface shading plants are submerged

Contrary to oft-quoted formulas, if the fish-load is kept on the low side, you can enjoy whatever plants you like in the garden.
Photo by H. Nash

aquatics that take most of their nutrients directly from the water through their leaves. We've never had episodes of green water in our ponds with one bunch per square

foot of water surface of these plants. (The plant we use is *Elodea canadensis*, a hardier version of the commonly available anacharis. This unique plant breaks dormancy approximately two weeks earlier than anacharis in our zone 5 area, right at the same time the algae blooms occur in other ponds around us.) Among our many ponds, we have clear water with no total-surface plantings and with no marginal plantings. We make sure to have a low fish count and enough submerged plants.

Many pondkeepers have achieved the same result with only surface floaters, primarily water hyacinth, whose long and dense roots remove nutrients directly from the water. A tropical plant, however, water hyacinth cannot be added to the cold-climate pond until the water has warmed in the spring and frost dangers have passed, a point often occurring after initial algae blooms.

It won't hurt your pond for you to follow the recommended formu-

Learning the Language

emergent plants—aquatic plants that grow rooted in submersed soil with their stems and leaves rising above the water (also known as marginal plants)
interveinal chlorosis—plant leaves turning yellow with the veins remaining green; an indication of excessive fertilizer
lotus—common name of plants of the *Nelumbo* family (as opposed to water lilies, which are members of the family *Nymphaea*), which grow emergent from water

marginal plants—aquatic plants that grow rooted in submersed soil, their stems and leaves rising above the water (also known as emergent plants)
pond balance—appropriate numbers of plants and fish to achieve clean and healthy water
rhizome—horizontal underground stems from which roots and shoots develop
submersed plants—plants that grow fully underwater
trace elements—minerals needed by plants in very minute quantities

las, but you really have much more latitude to plant your pond with the plants you most enjoy and desire. Michael Duff, for example, is an avid water lily collector. His ponds are fully covered with water lily leaves, as he always strives to fit in just one more lily specimen. Yet his waters are perfectly clear and healthy for his lovely fantails, comets, and black moors because he layers his pond bottoms with pea gravel, in which grow his submerged grasses, and he keeps the fish population under control.

THE TYPES OF AQUATIC PLANTS

1. Floating-leaf but rooted: These plants must be grown in a container of soil or directly in the soil of an earthen pond. They produce lengthened stems that reach the water surface where the leaves float. Water lilies and floating hearts are such plants.

Water hyacinths, considered noxious weeds in tropical zones, make lovely shade-producing and nutrient-removing plants for the water garden.   Photo by H. Nash

2. True floating plants: These plants produce trailing roots that directly take nutrients from the water. These roots may be quite profuse, as in water hyacinths, or barely visible, as in the tiny duckweed.
3. Marginal or emergent aquatic plants: These plants grow with their roots in soil in either very wet soil or in soil up to several inches deep over the plant's crown. They are also known as emergent plants

since their stems, leaves, and flowers extend out of the water. Cattails, arrowhead, and water irises are examples of these plants.
4. Submersed plants: These plants grow fully underwater. While they produce roots that both anchor and derive some nourishment from the soil, their primary food source is acquired by direct nutrient uptake through their submerged leaves.

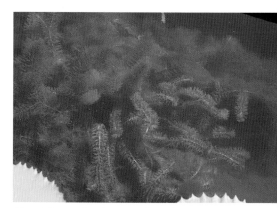

Certainly not the glamour plants in a pond, submerged grasses perform vital functions of water clarity and fish cover. Photo by H. Nash

With their rhizomes growing in submersed soil, water lilies send long stems to the surface, where their leaves and flowers float mystically.   Photo by H. Nash

Marginal or emergent aquatic plants send their stems, leaves, and flowers into the air above the water in which they grow.
Photo by H. Nash

ℳini-encyclopedia of commonly available plants

The following plants are commonly available at local nurseries and from mail-order businesses.

Hardy Water Lilies

N. 'Florida Sunset'
Photo by Perry D. Slocum

N. 'Mayla'
Photo by
H. Nash

N. 'Pink Grapefruit'
Photo by H. Nash

N. 'Lily Pons'
Photo by Perry D. Slocum

Tropical Water Lilies

N. 'Midnight'
Photo by H. Nash

N. 'Persian Lilac'
Photo by H. Nash

N. 'Leopardess'
Photo by H. Nash

N. 'Albert Greenberg'
Photo by H. Nash

Hardy Marginal Aquatic Plants

Sagittaria latifolia, *arrowhead*
Photo by H. Nash

Pontederia cordata,
pickerel weed
Photo by Marilyn Cook

Iris laevigata
'Variegata,' *variegated
Louisiana iris*
Photo by H. Nash

Myriophyllum
aquatica,
parrot's feather
Photo by H. Nash

Tropical Marginal Aquatic Plants

Canna
Photo by H. Nash

Esculenta, *Taro or elephant ear*
Photo by H. Nash

Nymphoides spp., *white snowflake*
Photo by H. Nash

Cyperus umbellatus, *umbrella palm*
Photo by Ron Everhart

Submerged Aquatic Plants

Floating Aquatic Plants

Ceratophyllum, *hornwort or coontail*
Photo by Ron Everhart

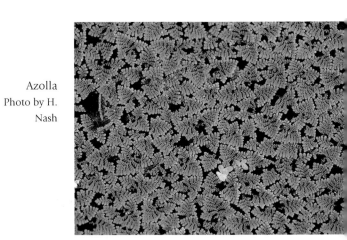

Azolla
Photo by H.
Nash

Potogeton,
curly pondweed
Photo by H.
Nash

Salvinia, *water fern*
Photo by H. Nash

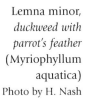

Cabomba, *showing
tiny surface bloom*
Photo by H. Nash

Lemna minor,
*duckweed with
parrot's feather*
(Myriophyllum
aquatica)
Photo by H. Nash

TAKING CARE OF YOUR POND PLANTS

During growing season, aquatic plants require minimal care. Very vigorous plants, especially floating plants, may require netting or occasional thinning. Fertilize plants monthly. If you use extend-release fertilizers, fertilize once or twice a season.

The busiest aquatic plant season is the spring, when plants need division and repotting. Aquatic plants are generally vigorous growers. If maintenance time is at a premium, select plants that do not grow as vigorously as others. Some growers have discovered that many aquatic plants do not need as much soil depth as was once thought. They have been growing the plants in squatter, wider pots. Likewise, growing plants in containers without drainage holes helps confine them. However, it is especially important to fertilize confined aquatic plants. Pots with holes or laundry-basket-type

Within a single season, aquatic plants may fill out their pots or jump out of them. Plants can be divided into the summer (although this is usually done in the spring) so long as their roots can establish before winter dormancy.   Photo by Ron Everhart

Since water lily leaves last only 2–3 weeks, prune away the yellow, aging leaves before they decompose and foul the water. Submerged grasses that become invasive should also be pruned back.
Photo by Ron Everhart

planters allow plant roots to escape and send up shoots elsewhere. Pond bottoms covered with pea gravel offer additional nutrients to these roots, though they require more intensive maintenance.

Planting Soil for Aquatics

The most commonly recommended soil for planting aquatics is heavy garden loam, soil with some clay content and good fertility. Additives such as peat or vermiculite are not used as they can float out of the soil and dirty the water. Certain aquatic plants, such as true bog plants like bog bean (*Menyanthese trifoliata*) and the callas (*Zantedeschia*), need peat or acid supplements in their potting mix. Most plants you will grow, however, do not need enhancement.

Many water gardeners add compost to their potting soil. For a wheelbarrow full of soil, add one or two shovels of composted cow or chicken manure. You can mix as much as 30 percent sand into your potting mix. Add 10-10-10 granular fertilizer at a rate of one part fertilizer to five parts of soil if you wish.

If you don't have a garden source for your aquatic plant soil, commercial preparations are now available, although one 40-pound bag services little more than one or two good-sized pots. For occasional repottings, these mixtures are handy.

Aquatic Plant Fertilizer

If you repot your plants in fresh soil each spring, they will survive without supplemental feeding. But if you want the plants to flourish

Calla lilies (Zantedeschia) *are one of the few plants to grow in your pond that are happiest with some acid added to their soil.* Bog bean (Menyanthes) *and Louisiana irises are others.*   Photo by H. Nash

with maximum growth and bloom, regular feeding is required. Whatever brand you use, do not use compositions with more than 10 percent nitrogen or you risk burning the plants. Place the fertilizer in the bottom portion of the pot so the plant roots have to look for it. Push subsequent feedings into the soil a few inches from the plant crown. Cover the hole with soil to prevent the fertilizer from leaching back into the pond water. A recent innovation in aquatic plant fertilizers is the extend-release tab. These tablets also contain trace elements. Usually, twice as many are used as the traditional tabs, but you may need to reapply only once more during the growing season, if at all.

General Potting Guidelines

1. Consider soil and planting-depth requirements of the plant. To avoid excessively heavy pots, use the least amount of soil necessary.
2. Place fertilizer tabs in the bottom of the pot.
3. Use slightly moistened soil and tamp it around the plant roots to avoid air pockets that might bubble the plant out of the pot.
4. Set the plant in at its appropriate depth.
5. Cover the soil with gravel topping. While pea gravel is commonly used, it is too small to discourage even large goldfish from rooting around in it and disturbing your plants. One- to two-inch river rock may work better.

Potting a Lotus

Because of the vigorous running nature of their tubers, lotuses are usually potted in wide, shallow containers. Dwarf varieties, such as 'Momo Botan' and 'Chawan Basu,' should be planted in containers of at least 24 in (60 cm) in diameter with 10–12 in (25–30 cm) of depth. Standard-size lotuses do best in containers 3 feet (90 cm) in diameter. Planting these gorgeous plants in smaller containers crowds them, resulting in fewer or no blooms. These containers will accommodate the plants for one to two years. Because these containers are much larger and less manageable than containers used for other aquatic plants, lotuses are often planted in individual containers that also serve as their ponds.

Although you can buy lotuses already potted from garden centers, many people order bareroot tubers by mail for planting in April and May. Most nurseries will not mail lotus tubers after May. The primary cause of lotus tuber failure is transplant shock caused by water that is too cold. Ideally, place the container on top of the ground in a sunny location until 5 to 6 leaves rise above the water, at which time the container can be moved into the pond just below the surface.

Another cause of tuber failure is that the growing tip breaks. Planting the tuber in a square or corrugated-sided container that allows the tip to grow into a corner is one cause. Smooth-sided, round containers avoid this risk.

Most printed sources characterize lotuses as heavy feeders. However, when potting a new, single rhizome, too much fertilizer can burn the plant, and the plant's leaves turn yellow around the remaining green veins (interveinal chlorosis). An established plant of a year of more can be fed more heavily, as often as the recommended 3–4 weeks during the growing season. Because growing tips of lotuses are brittle, prominent lotus hybridizer and grower Perry D. Slocum recommends not feeding them during their most active growing period, to avoid inserting fertilizer tabs and accidentally breaking off any growing tips.

Potting a Lotus Tuber

1. Space six aquatic tabs (10-15-10) evenly around the bottom of a 23-inch (60-cm) wide and 10-inch (25-cm) deep pot. Place 5 inches (12.5 cm) of dirt in the container. Any more dirt is unnecessary and may result in a container too heavy to move.

2. Place the lotus tuber on top of the dirt with the cut edge of the rhizome against the edge of the pot.

3. Place a flat rock on top of the tuber and gently fill the container so that 2–3 in (5–7.5 cm) of water covers the tuber. You can also cover the tuber with a shallow layer of soil, taking care to keep the growing tip free of soil. Keep the container in a warm, sunny place as the plant establishes itself. Add water as necessary to compensate for evaporation. Once the lotus has produced several leaves, a shallow layer of soil may be added to cover the tuber, always with care not to cover the growing tip. Gravel topping may also be added in the same manner, if desired.

Potting Water Lilies

Division and potting of hardy water lilies vary according to the type of rhizome or rootstock of the particular variety. Four types of rootstock are commonly recognized in the family of *Nymphaea*: mexicana, odorata, tuberosa, and marliac. Odorata rhizomes grow into thick, fleshy, horizontally extended forms with growing eyes along the length of the tuber that develop into thick branches if not trimmed away. Leaves and flowers are produced from these growing tips.

Tuberosa rhizomes are characterized by broomstick-thin horizontal growths with rapidly growing eyes along the length that easily snap free. Leaves and flower stems are produced along the rhizome rather than from a specific growing tip or eye.

Marliac-type rhizomes, while tending toward horizontal growth, are less vigorous than the odorata or tuberosa types. Plantsmen often characterize their growth as more "clumping" than "running." A variation of the marliac rhizome is distinguished by some growers as a fifth type of rhizome, the thumb or finger rhizome, the name reflecting the miniature version of the rhizome.

Tropical water lilies and some hardy water lilies grow from rhizomes with an upright growth habit, often compared to a small pineapple form and called a mexicana type. New plants form from tubers either immediately under or immediately adjacent to the tuber. (Night-blooming tropicals form their tubers embedded within the mother tuber.)

Tuberosa rhizome

Odorata rhizome

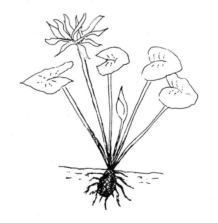

Tropical rhizome
Drawings by Marilyn Cook

General Potting Procedure for Hardy Water Lilies

Prepare the water lily rhizome for potting: To repot a water lily from your own mother plant, use a sharp knife to trim away excess roots and cut the furled leaves' stems close to the rhizome. (If you will immediately return the plant to the pond, you need not remove so many of the leaves; do your repotting in a shady place and keep the plant covered with wet newspapers until it can be returned to the pond.) Trim the rhizome to no more than 2 or 3 inches (5 to 7.5 cm) long. Discard the oldest portion of the rhizome that appears hollow and dead. Any growing points on the rhizome can be separated in this manner. You may find several sections capable of producing a blooming plant on a single mother plant. Even rooted growing eyes can be potted in small pots to grow until they are large enough for moving into larger pots.

Mail-order plants that are received bare root should be checked that any leaves and roots left on them are still fresh and without injury and/or rot. Trim away any damage. New growth is sent out quickly from the rhizome.

To pot odorata and tuberosa type rhizomes, *Nuphar*, and water hawthorne *(Aponogeton)*:

1. Use as large a pot as you can manage, at least 5-gallon (20-l). Space one aquatic plant tab per gallon (4 l) of soil evenly around the bottom of the container.

2. Fill the pot three-quarters full with dampened potting mix, mounding the soil slightly for the rhizome so that it can be placed at a 45° angle with the cut edge against the side wall of the pot and the growing tip pointing into the center of the pot. This will give the rhizome maximum growing room across the pot.

3. If the rhizome still has viable roots attached to it, spread them across the soil.

4. Fill the remaining space in the container with soil, tamping it to ensure root contact and minimal air spaces. Leave the growing tip free of soil.

5. Top with an inch (2.5 cm) of river stone kept free of the growing tip.

6. Gently lower the potted plant into the pond water to the desired depth. Usually a freshly potted plant is placed with shallow water over the pot until leaf production indicates roots have established. The plant can then be moved to its normal depth. If, however, you have retained long-stemmed leaves and roots on the plant, it can be set in its normal depth.

An alternate method of planting a well-trimmed rhizome is to fill the pot full of soil and have it submerged in water. Simply wiggle in the trimmed rhizome at the edge of the pot until the soil covers all but the growing tip.

Wash the lily rhizome to determine points of division.
Photos by Ron Everhart

Cut the rhizome into two-inch sections, each with a growing tip.

Set the cut end of the rhizome against a side wall of the pot and cover all but the growing tip with soil. Top with gravel to prevent soil escaping into the water.

Planting Tropical Water Lilies, Mexicana-Type Rhizomes, Water Snowflakes and Floating Hearts (Nymphoides)—A Fast Planting Method

Trim the rhizome of all roots and leaves.
Photos by H. Nash

With fertilizer tabs in the pot bottom, fill pots with soil and submerge them in shallow water.

Wiggle the trimmed rhizome into the pot. Place the cut edge of hardy lily rhizomes against the side wall.

1. Plant these rhizomes in the center of your pot since they are upright growers. Follow the same procedure of plant and pot preparation listed above.

2. Tropical water lily rhizomes are planted with the crown of the plant just above the soil level. Most growers recommend 5-gallon pots. Do not set out tropical water lilies until the water temperature has stabilized at 70°F (20°C). Night-blooming tropical plants should not be set out until water temperatures have stabilized closer to 75° degrees.

An alternate method of planting a well-trimmed tropical water lily is to fill the pot full of soil and then scoop out a section in the center of the pot. Tuck in the rhizome and tamp it into the soil, again with the crown above the soil level. A flat rock may be needed to help hold the rhizome in place until growth is established.

Potting Submerged Plants

Submerged plants are either bunching plants or rooted plants. Bunching plants, such as anacharis, *Elodea*, and *Cabomba*, are usually sold in bunches of stem cuttings with a lead strip wrapped around the base. They may be tossed into the pond and allowed to sink. As long as they sink to the pond bottom, they will grow. Plants that become unanchored and float to the surface may turn mushy and die, especially in hot and sunny conditions.

Since these bunching plants do form roots primarily for anchoring, they can be potted. Receiving most of their nutrients directly from the water, they can be potted in gravel rather than in soil. Simply fill a container two-thirds full of gravel, lay the plants into the pot, and anchor their roots with more gravel.

Hornwort (*Ceratophyllum*) is a plant that floats just below the surface. During the winter, it usually drifts to the pond bottom, where it remains until the following spring. It requires no potting.

Other submerged plants, such as tape grass or cork-screw grass (*Vallisneria*) or dwarf sagittaria (*Sagittaria natans*), are shallow rooters that spread by stolons through the surface of the soil. Both of these species are planted in shallow pots or trays of soil. Either sand or pea gravel can be used as topping over the soil. While *Vallisneria* usually establishes in the presence of fish, dwarf Sagittaria, especially young plants, proves too tasty to both koi and goldfish to

Elodea canadensis, *a submerged grass, derives most of its nutrients directly from its leaves and so can be planted in pots of gravel.*   Photo by Ron Everhart

establish without protection. Either provide netting over the container itself or set up an area of the pond with inconspicuous black plastic netting to protect the plants from the fish.

An effective planting method that requires control is planting the submerged grasses, such as dwarf sagittaria, directly into a layer of gravel on the pond bottom.
Photo by Ron Everhart

Potting Marginal or Emergent Aquatic Plants

Marginal plants display two basic growing habits: upright and clumping or horizontal and running. The growing habit determines the method of potting.

Upright emergents, such as bulrushes (*Scirpus*), grow from clumping rhizomes that are best potted in the center of the container with the plant's crown at the soil's surface. These plants can be grown in traditional pots.

Fast-traveling, horizontal rhizomes are found in water irises, pickerel, cattails, and sweet flags. Standard nursery containers are usually "jumped" before the end of the growing season. In the wild, the rhizomes or stolons of these plants creep along the surface of the soil. Provide a wide-mouthed pot to accommodate this growth habit. Place the cut rhizome up against the side of the pot so that maximum room is given for growth across the pot. If

you do not have enough roots to anchor the plant, use a flat rock to hold it in place until it establishes. Coarse sand or river rock prevents fish from making the water murky as they root around the plants.

Running type of horizontal growth is seen in plants such as bog bean (*Menyanthes*), floating heart and water snowflakes (*Nymphoides*), and in water clover (*Marsilea*). Although started by rooting within a container of soil, these plants send out vigorous runners across the surface of the water. Roots form along the runners and anchor the plants in any available pots. Bog bean tends not to be so vigorous in most ponds because it requires acid in its soil. The others, however, can become major problems if not controlled and thinned. These plants are potted in wide-mouthed pots with shallow soil. Upon potting, weight the plant across the top of the soil.

Clump-growing marginals, such as Scirpus *or bulrush, are divided into squares of roots and plant tops. Plant them in the center of their pots.*
Photo by Ron Everhart

*Fleshy rooted plants, such as pickerel (*Pontederia*), leave behind a space-consuming mass of dead rhizome from the previous year. Separate the fresh growth and repot it.*   Photo by Ron Everhart

*To pot running plants, such as bog bean (*Menyanthes*) or water clovers (*Marsilea*), lay a rooted cutting across a shallow pot of soil, lightly cover the roots, and anchor the cutting with a flat rock until it establishes.*
Photo by H. Nash

Sweetflags grow from a running surface root that easily jumps a standard nursery pot in a single season. Plant them in wide-mouthed pots with the cut end of the rhizome against the pot wall for maximum growing room.   Photo by Ron Everhart

Running-type plants do not require much soil.   Photo by H. Nash

CHAPTER FIVE

Fish in the Water Garden

❧

KOI VS. GOLDFISH

Too often, a new pond owner visits the local pet store and announces, "I've got a new pond, and I want some fish!" Inexperienced pet store employees point to a large tank and say, "You want koi! That's a pond fish." Koi really are the classic—they are glamour pond fish. Although some experts proclaim that koi don't need anything more than goldfish, koi do have special needs and not every water garden can accommodate them.

Koi grow much larger than goldfish. A mature goldfish may be 9 inches long under ideal conditions, but a koi will grow to at least twice that—sometimes even three times as long. Koi need more pond space than goldfish.

Goldfish can survive in fairly shallow water and in indoor aquariums. Koi, however, require depths in excess of 2½ feet for optimal health. Most koi experts recommend no less than 3 feet of depth, with 4 to 6 feet commonly suggested.

Young koi may not disturb your aquatic plants, but larger koi need vegetables in their diet. They consider your submerged aquatics a salad bar! Goldfish may nibble on your submerged grasses and on the roots of your water hyacinths, and they may even decimate your water lettuce, but, unlike koi, they are not likely to keep you running to the pond shop for replacement plants. Many fish root around in the soil for tasty larvae. A goldfish's nose is considerably smaller and lacking in the pushing power of a koi's. Koi may uproot your plants or bare their roots.

Although koi and goldfish can coexist peacefully in a pond, each breed's needs should be met to ensure their best health.
Photo by H. Nash

If your pond is large enough and deep enough to keep koi healthy, there are ways to adapt it to both koi and plants. Many koi enthusiasts end up with a double-pond setup, so a deeper and minimally planted pond supports the koi and a second pond serves the plants...and a few goldfish. A medium-size pond can accommodate butterfly koi, a member of the koi family with long flowing fins and tail. Since butterfly koi commonly grow to 16 inches or more, plan on adequate room.

It is unfair to keep fish in conditions that cannot promote good health and survival. If you can supply a healthy environment, by all means, indulge yourself.

THE GOLDEN ORFE

Many new pondkeepers, hearing that the golden orfe is a "surface feeder," set out on a quest to stock this fish in their ponds to control insects. Actually, the orfe is a surface *schooling* fish, which means you must have several of them for their best health and well-being. Quite active swimmers darting rapidly around the pond, they need

plenty of room. All this, plus a mature size of 18 to 24 inches in length, means a larger pond habitat is necessary for this breed.

Orfe are also more sensitive to water quality and are particularly susceptible to problems due to chemicals. Goldfish, koi, and many other breeds also swim near the water surface and eat both insects and food that you float to them. Orfe can be a delightful addition to your pond if you are certain you have the proper conditions to satisfy a whole school of them.

NATIVE FISH

Keeping native fish, like keeping domesticated ones, presents habitat considerations. Catfish, for example, have the reputation of being scavengers. Great, you think, the perfect fish to keep the pond bottom free of debris. Wrong. It means they root around the pond bottom to feed. Mulm on the pond bottom will be continually stirred up. Catfish grow to considerable lengths and require more depth for optimum survival than the typical water garden usually presents. (The tropical catfish, the *Plecostomus*,

Learning the Language

blushing—in fish, a pink-to-reddish cast on the fins and tail indicating stress, often caused by ammonia or nitrite poisoning

butterfly koi—a variation of the classic koi; bearing long, flowing fins and tails; they grow up to 18–22 inches long

daphnia—commonly called water fleas, these nearly microscopic free-swimmers are relished by fish for food and cause no harm to water gardens

feeder goldfish—goldfish bred in quantity as food for other predacious fish

fry—baby fish

golden orfe—a narrow-bodied, surface-schooling fish that grows 18 to 22 inches long.

goldfish—a cold-water pond fish, available in various colors of orange to red; other breeds include fantails, calicos, as well as exotic breeds better suited to the indoor aquarium; generally grows no longer than 8 to 10 inches

hibernation—in fish, a necessary period of reduced metabolism and rest when water temperature falls below 45 degrees

koi—a long-lived member of the carp family, koi are famous for their magnificent colors and their many generations of breeding by the Japanese, growing to 24 inches long or more

life cycle—the complete cycle of a parasite, from introduction to the pond as an egg, through nymph stages, host stages, free-swimming stages, encysted, and parasitic stages; many parasites are not vulnerable during specific stages of their life cycle

mulm—fine particles of organic and inorganic matter that accumulate on the pond bottom

native fish—fish commonly found in natural lakes and ponds, such as minnows, blue gill, and bass

organic debris—fish and plant wastes that collect on the pond bottom and decompose anaerobically, producing fish-toxic by-products of hydrogen sulfide and methane gases

parasites—microscopic-size animals, such as anchor worm and fish lice, that feed on their fish hosts

predacious fish—fish that feed upon other fish

predators—animals such as raccoons, blue herons, egrets, and kingfishers that prey upon pond fish

scavenger fish—bottom-feeding fish, such as catfish

spawning—term to describe fish breeding

however, can spend summers in your pond. Be prepared to bring him back inside before the water chills too much in the fall. Although this fellow can survive in an indoor fish tank at room temperature, he won't make it through the winter in water below 50 degrees!)

Predacious fish, such as bass, require both depth and small fish for food, thereby ruling them out as pet pond fish. Some native species, however, such as minnows or blue gill, can be adapted to water garden life. They do not give life and color to the garden the way goldfish do. We've had blue gill in one of our ponds for several years now. (We didn't put them there on purpose; they were a present from a duck.) With the pea gravel bottom in that pond, blue gill find ample nesting areas and have proliferated to the point of taking over the entire pond. We suspect that blue gill require greater water depth in the winter than what is offered by the traditional water garden, as we had a massive blue gill fish-kill following a severe winter, even though the koi and goldfish survived. Minnows, particularly the rosy reds, seem to be quite sensitive to cold and may not survive in the cold climate winter pond. They are easily wintered in an aquarium.

If you wish to keep native fish in your water garden, check at fish hatcheries or with your state's department of fish and wildlife to be certain you can successfully meet their needs.

GOLDFISH—THE EASIEST TO KEEP!

Goldfish really are the easiest to keep of any pond fish. They don't grow too big, and they're not too fussy about water quality (although high ammonia and nitrite will kill them, as they will any other fish). Goldfish are colorful and fun to watch in the pond, and they aren't too expensive.

Because they are prolific breeders and easy to tend, goldfish are grown in many hatcheries as food for other fish. Consequently, their health is not attended to carefully. For that reason, be especially observant in selecting the fish you put in your pond. A fish with parasites or disease, for example, will contaminate the pond and guarantee a frustrating and sad ongoing battle.

When you look at the fish in the pet store, first check the overall health of the tank. If even one fish is isolated, has his fins clamped to his body, or shows signs of problems, such as cloudy eyes, red sores, white spots, or ragged fins, avoid *all* fish in that tank unless you are prepared to keep your seemingly healthy selections in a quarantine fish tank at home until you can be sure they are healthy. (Many parasite and disease life cycles require up to two weeks to show themselves.) It is always a good idea to quarantine any new fish until you are certain they are perfectly healthy and free of problems. Treating sick fish is much less expensive in a 10-gallon aquarium than in a 1000-gallon pond. If you are fortunate enough to have a friend who already has a pond, chances are your friend may

When you purchase goldfish, check the health of the entire tank.
Photo by H. Nash

have a few extra healthy fish to share with you.

As you explore the world of goldfish, you'll find quite a few varieties that are perfect pond pets in your new garden. The common goldfish is generally orange with a short tail and short fins. The comet goldfish, however, has a more slender body and long fins and tail. Comets in a bright red-orange color brighten up any pond.

Note that fish of 1 to 3 inches in length displaying attractive black or white splotches are not likely to retain their patterns. Goldfish are hatched in dull, drab colors that allow the tiny babies to blend into their surroundings. Their colors may continue to change over several years. Black is a particularly transitional color. Fish with white splotches may develop into fully white fish by the time the color change is completed. Myth has it that white goldfish are weaker than their more colorful counterparts, but we have noticed no such distinction.

We like including a white fish in the pond as a barometer of fish health. When a fish is stressed by

Goldfish can be prolific breeders.
Photo by H. Nash

invisibly rising ammonia levels that can lead quickly to rising and deadly nitrite presence, the fish displays a "blushing" in the fins and tail. This blush is not as obvious in a fish with colored fins as it is in a white fish. The blushing reddens and spreads into the fish's body as the stress increases. The final stage of nitrite poisoning is characterized by distinctive red veining on the fish's body. When you see the fins acquiring a rosy blush, test the water for ammonia and nitrite.

Fantail goldfish can be an attractive addition to your pond. These deep-bodied fish have flowing tails and an unspeakable grace of movement in the water. They offer a range of colors, including calico. Note that deep-bodied fish do not compete well for food with more agile fish. Also, exotic fantail goldfish, such as the oranda with its bubbled cap or fish with protruding or bubbled eyes, are less tolerant of extremely cold water. These fish need to be wintered indoors. The dorsel-less varieties such as the lionhead cannot compete at all with other fish for food in the outdoor pond. Traditional fantails, however, and even classy black moors make delightful pond pets.

BASIC FISH BEHAVIOR AND CARE IN THE WATER GARDEN

As your pond slumbers through the winter with water temperatures below 50 degrees, your fish experience a sort of hibernation, too. Because their metabolisms are too slow during this cold period to be able to digest food, do not feed

During the cold winter months, koi and goldfish metabolisms slow and fish go into a rest period, living off their stored body fat. Photo by H. Nash

What you feed your fish is temperature-dependent—high protein foods during warm months and high carbohydrate foods during early spring and autumn. Photo by H. Nash

Provide submerged grasses to give cover to tiny fry. Larger adult fish and frogs will feed on them. Photo by H. Nash

The shubunkin, a calico goldfish, offers unique blue coloration. Photo by H. Nash

them. Their activity is minimal as they survive by burning stored body fat. Do not feed them even on the occasional warm day when they lazily glide about the pond surface.

In the spring, the water begins to warm. Using a pond thermometer, monitor the temperature 10 to 12 inches below the surface. Once the temperature stabilizes around 50 degrees, resume feeding your finned pets. In deference to their still-slow metabolisms, feed them easily digestible foods, such as wheat-germ-based floating pellets. Feed them lightly these first two weeks, always in the mornings, to allow ample digestive time before temperatures fall again at night.

With their immune systems suppressed over the winter months, watch closely for any signs of parasites or disease as your pets resume their surface feedings. This is the time of year when they are most vulnerable to attack. If you notice signs of problems, net out the affected fish for a stint in the hospital tank indoors with appropriate treatment.

Changing water temperatures trigger spawning instincts in fish. Goldfish will spawn when they are 3 inches long. One early spring morning my daughter phoned me in a panic: her goldfish had turned aggressive and were chasing each other around the pond; they were bumping one another and aggressively pursuing certain fatter fish, even beaching the pursued fish. It was my daughter's first experience with spawning fish.

During this period, keep a close eye in the early morning to be sure that any beached females are returned safely to the water. Also, watch for any abrasions on the fish that might become infected. Consider removing any sharp objects from the pond temporarily.

Within a few days the eggs hatch into needle-thin fry. The larger fish will eat not only their own eggs but also their own babies. This is Nature's way of controlling the population. (Frogs help with this chore, too.) As the babies begin to grow, you may wish to add flake food or balls of cooked oatmeal to your feeding regimen for them. Nature provides food for them, too: water fleas or daphnia appear in the water during this period, along with tiny mosquito larvae and other microscopic organisms.

Once the water has warmed above 55 degrees, resume feeding normal high-protein food. Depending on how much natural food is available in your garden, you may need to feed your fish as often as three times a day during the summer months. Your fish are active, nosing about in your plants' gravel toppings, nibbling on submerged grasses, and swimming about. Occasionally they may leap out of the water, but this will not happen very frequently. If you notice them leaping out of the water, check the ammonia and nitrite levels to make sure everything is okay. Check to see if the problem is electrical current in the pond from a power source that runs your pump or lighting.

Don't be surprised if your fish spawn more than once during the summer season. I recall one year when our goldfish spawned every three weeks throughout the summer, probably because of erratic weather patterns that caused fluctuating pond water temperatures. Spawning is often prompted by changes in water temperature, hence the spring spawning.

As autumn approaches and the water temperature begins to cool, switch back to the wheat-germ-based feeding regimen. Begin tapering off the amount of food as the appetite of your fish decreases. A good rule of thumb is to feed only what they will eat in 5 to 10 minutes. Net out any food they do not eat during this period so that it doesn't rot in the pond and foul the water. Stop feeding altogether once the water temperature stabilizes below 50 degrees. If predators such as raccoons or herons are a problem, put overturned pots in the pond bottom as winter hiding places for your fish when plants are dormant and protective cover is minimized.

If you have a submersible pump running in the pond, move it to the surface and disconnect the fittings so it will bubble and keep a hole open in the ice. Use a skimmer net or pond vac to remove excess organic debris from the pond bottom before the weather turns too cold. This will prevent fish-toxic gases from being generated by anaerobic decomposition. Unless your pond is overstocked with fish, you will not need to keep aeration going through the winter months. However, if you do supply aeration, be sure it is supplied only in the top third of the pond water. Water remains warmest at the bottom of the pond, where the fish spend most of their time during the winter; you don't want to alter that warmer temperature by recycling colder surface water into it. A worst case scenario is that the pond could freeze solid to the bottom!

A SICK FISH?

Common Fish Diseases

Dropsy—also called pine-cone disease because the fish scales protrude from the body due to pressure of accumulated body fluids. It is bacterial, but does not seem to be infectious, although it is often fatal. Treat with antibiotics.

Foam disease—Fish appear to be floating on their side and covered with air bubbles. Caused by excess oxygen in excessively green water (algae); aerate the water and/or move fish into fresh water. Treat for algae and reduce the number of fish in the pond.

Flukes—two varieties of trematode worms parasitic to fish: gill flukes (*Dactylogyrus*) and skin flukes (*Gyrodactylus*). Barely visible, they produce symptoms including scraping against objects, fidgety fins, or quick mouth opening and closing. Treat with proprietary medication in a hospital tank.

Fungus—*Saprolengnia* spp, or water musk disease, produces cottony growths on skin, especially around mouth, fins and tail, and occurs most often in colder water of spring, autumn, and winter. Use malachite green or copper sulfate to treat in a hospital tank, closely observing dosage as excess can be deadly to fish.

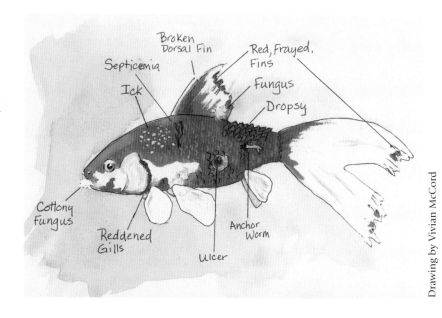

Drawing by Vivian McCord

Ich—*Ichthyophthirius multifiliis*, commonly known as white spot disease, is caused by a parasite, producing white specks on the fish's body. When the spots spread to the head and gills, the fish has difficulty breathing and dies. Treat with salt; gradually raise the water temperature to 76° F, increase aeration, and add one teaspoon of salt for each quart of water in the tank. Advanced cases may involve leaving the fish in a container with half a teaspoon of quinine sulfate per gallon of water for three weeks. Malachite green can be used, too, according to directions.

Anchor worm—*Lernaea carassii* has a head shaped like a ship's anchor that allows it to burrow into a fish's body, usually near the fins or tail. The worm looks like a tiny white stick protruding from the fish. Irritation produces a bloody red spot. Remove very carefully with tweezers, swabbing the site with mercurochrome. Treat the pond three times in early spring with

Dipterex at seven-day intervals, to accommodate the parasite's life cycle. Anchor worms are treatable in water only during the free-swimming stage.

Fish lice—*Argulus* sp. fasten themselves flat against the body of the fish and are not noticeable. Check for them if your fish are rubbing themselves against objects. Dipterex is effective when used as for anchor worms. You can also pat the fish with a swab of half-and-half solution of kerosene and turpentine to remove them. Always rinse the fish well after such treatments.

Setting Up the Hospital/Quarantine Tank

A glass aquarium may be set up as a hospital or quarantine tank. Equip it with at least an aeration device, usually an air pump with an air stone attached. A recirculating filter may be used, but it

A simple ten-gallon glass aquarium equipped with aeration serves as a hospital tank.   Photo by Oliver Jackson

should be equipped with only ammonia-absorbing media and filter floss or foam if you are using medications in the tank. Activated carbon, commonly used in aquarium filters, will immediately filter or adsorb any medications from the water. To determine the fish-holding capacity of the aquarium, compute the area of the tank in square inches. Divide this figure by 30 to determine the number of body inches the tank can accommodate. Since overcrowding is also stressful, do not add to the distress of an already stressed or diseased fish. Provide a cover to the tank to prevent fish from jumping out.

In moving your fish between quarters, provide for water temperature changes that will not further stress them.
Photo by Ron Everhart

Use a thermometer to verify the tank's water temperature, important in medicating the fish as well as determining transport method when you are ready to return the fish to the pond.
Photo by Oliver Jackson

If the fish must be housed in the tank for any length of time, using a filter may be advisable. Zeolite, a white mineral, can be used to remove ammonia from the tank water. Carbon removes physical impurities and medication from the water; do not use if medicating.
Photo by Oliver Jackson

Other Hardy Cold-Water Fish for Your Pond

Calico fantail goldfish.
Photo courtesy of Blue Ridge Fish Hatchery

Butterfly koi.
Photo courtesy of Blue Ridge Fish Hatchery

Red-cap oranda goldfish.
Photo courtesy of Blue Ridge Fish Hatchery

CHAPTER SIX

Pumps & Filters

If you plan to move water in your pond, whether by waterfall, stream, fountain, or spouting ornament, you will need a pump. This requires an electrical outlet. Have a protected conduit installed in the ground and use a low-voltage transformer with a ground fault circuit interrupter to ensure safety. Before installing, check local ordinances. Outdoor extension cords loose upon the ground are both unsightly and unsafe.

Pumps are available in both submersible and external, out-of-pond models. The smallest pumps are most economical in the submersible models, while larger pumps are presently more economically run in the external models. At the same time, external, more economical pumps are more expensive to buy than submersible models. Over the life of your water garden, however, the saving in cost of operation negates the cost differential.

THE SUBMERSIBLE PUMP

Placed directly in the pond, the submersible pump is elevated from the actual bottom of the pond to prevent silt and debris from clogging the unit. Water is pumped directly from the pond by way of piping to the moving water feature. Commonly known as sump pumps, these pumps are free of distracting noise and are useful for draining the pond when necessary.

The major disadvantage of a submersible pump is its relative inaccessibility. Filter attachments and screens require regular cleaning, especially in early spring and fall. The pump can be set within a plastic mesh basket to make retrieval easier.

A mechanical filter (a screen barrier) prevents particulate matter and debris from hampering pump operation. If these screens or filters

Most people think of a standard swimming pool sand filter when they think of an out-of-pond pump system.   Photo by H. Nash

require cleaning more than once a week, you need additional screening area for the pump. Neglecting to keep media clean enough for the pump to operate efficiently can have bad results. Very dirty filter media allows anaerobic bacteria to work on the collected waste matter and produce the fish-toxic gases hydrogen chloride and methane. When these gases form, they can cause the pump to separate from its filter attachment or cause the entire setup to float to the surface. Noticeable reduction in water flow indicates a need to clean the unit before this happens.

Another disadvantage of many submersible models is that the pump seals can rupture, sending oil coolant into the water. An oil slick on the water surface is unsightly and prevents surface gas exchanges, thereby endangering fish. A recent introduction in the pump market is the magnetic-drive pump, which avoids the use of oil coolants. At this time, these models are more expensive than traditional designs, but they are less expensive to operate.

For the smaller pond, a submersible pump may be the most efficient and carefree pump choice.   Photo by Oliver Jackson

THE EXTERNAL PUMP

When you think of an out-of-pond pump, chances are you envision the traditional swimming pool sand filter unit. While some pond-keepers do use such units, the weekly to daily maintenance makes them impractical for most people. A pond has far more organic particulate matter than a chemically maintained swimming pool. Sand is a fine medium that quickly clogs with such debris. "Channeling," in which water runs in limited paths, avoiding most of the filtration media, often occurs so that daily or frequent backwashing is required. Some pondkeepers have adapted these units by using larger media, such as a proportion of gravel. But gravel is heavy and difficult to clean.

Special external or centrifugal pumps made especially for ponds offer accessibility for routine maintenance and repairs. These pumps are housed somewhere near the water feature.

PUMP SIZES

Pumps are sized by gallons per hour (GPH) output at one foot of lift or height. Larger-capacity pumps are rated by horsepower (hp). Manufacturers offer charts that break down the power of each size pump according to incremental heights of one foot. While some manufacturers label pumps by GPH, others assign letter or number designations that require cross-referencing to charts.

Learning the Language

anaerobic bacteria—bacteria that work in oxygen-free environments to decompose organic matter

biological filtration—using bacteria to convert ammonia into nitrite and then into nitrate for good water quality in the presence of fish or heavy organic loads in the pond

biomechanical filters—filters that combine mechanical or particulate filtration with biological filtration

buoyant beads—small plastic beads used in a new filter design that by water pressure stay suspended in the system, discouraging debris accumulation while being colonized freely by bacteria

channeling—water running in limited paths and avoiding most of the filter media because of clogging by particle matter

chemical filtration—use of zeolite and/or carbon to filter the pond water

conduit—a tube for electric wires

down-flow systems—filters in which water enters the top and flows down through media to exit the system at the bottom

external pump—one that is used outside the pond

fluidized bed—adaptation of the buoyant bead concept using fine silica sand held in suspension by water flowing at high pressure

foam—even-textured synthetic filter media, similar in appearance to a kitchen sponge

gravity-fed—flowing into the filter system by the force of gravity. A pump then returns the water to the pond.

gravity-return—flowing from the filter system back into the pond by the force of gravity. A pump brings the water to the filter system from the pond.

GPH—gallons per hour, the measure used for most water garden pumps

ground fault circuit interrupter—a device that connects the electrical circuit to the ground and automatically shuts off the electrical flow, preventing electrical shocks

high pressure filters—compactly designed high-powered units such as swimming pool sand filters; used in newer designs such as buoyant bead systems

horizontal flow—flow of water through a system by entering one side, flowing across media, and exiting

To determine the pump required for your project, estimate the vertical height from the top of your pump to the top of your waterfall/stream. Add another foot of height or lift for every 10 feet of hosing required to take water from the pump to the top of the feature. This allows for loss of volume from resistance within the pipe.

For a reasonable flow of water, a general rule of thumb is to figure your waterfall/stream requirement as 150 gallons per hour per inch width of the spillway or channel.

For example, if your stream or waterfall spillway will be 10 inches wide, you will need a pump that produces a flow of 1500 gallons per hour (at whatever combined height of the feature and another foot of height for every ten feet of hosing to get there). In consulting the pump charts, follow down the column that corresponds to the height of your feature until you find the closest figure to the gallons per hour you need. Should your requirement fall between two sizes, select the larger. Using a

valve, you can adjust the pump flow to what you want. You cannot, however, increase pump capacity.

PLUMBING

The two main choices of piping to carry water from your pond to the water feature are rigid pipe or flexible tubing. Rigid PVC pipe is the least expensive, but it requires glued elbows and adapters to join everything together. Always use the white form of PVC, as water run through it is potable and safe for fish.

the opposite side of the unit

hp—horsepower; a measure used for larger capacity pumps

low-pressure filters—systems that rely on a slowed water movement through them to allow for particle settlement and/or biological filtration. Often these systems are gravity-fed or gravity-return systems.

low-voltage transformer—a device that changes electricity to a lower and safer voltage

magnetic drive pump—a pump that functions without oil coolant

matting—synthetic filter media available in sheets of varying thickness, similar to foam but coarser

mechanical filter—a barrier that prevents particulate matter from cycling through a pump

nitrogen cycle—the natural cycle within the pond, converting ammonia to nitrite, which is then converted to nitrate by bacterial activity

oil coolant—typically used in smaller-capacity pumps; chambers of oil keep the mechanical parts from overheating

organic load—the animals, plant life, and organic matter in the pond; primarily fish and decomposing organic matter

phyto-filtration—the use of plants to remove excess nutrients from the water and aid in particulate set-

tlement; also known as vegetative filtration

planktonic algae—single-celled, free-floating algae that makes the water appear thick and green like pea soup

pump—a machine that forces fluid through a piped system

PVC—rigid plastic used for piping

settling tanks—usually conical in shape; used before the bio-filtration unit in filtration systems to settle out particulate matter with slow-moving water

submersible pump—one that is used fully immersed in water

trickle filters—using larger synthetic media, like plastic hair curlers and a spray bar, to allow water to trickle down through the system

UVC—ultraviolet clarifiers, quartz sleeve-protected ultraviolet-light units that kill parasites and green water algae in water slowly moving by them

under-gravel filters—system that relies on the flow of water through a layer of gravel before being drawn from the pond and recycled

up-flow system—water flows down an oxygenating tower at the top of the system to the bottom of the unit into an open cavity where it swirls around to percolate back up through the media for exit near the top

Since PVC is a plastic, multiple-component silicones, epoxies, and superglues will attack and degrade it. Use single-component silicone for gluing any joints and adapters. Most single-component silicones contain acetic acid, which smells like vinegar. Acetic acid is corrosive to brass, copper, and bronze. If the joints you must glue will come into contact with any of these metals, use neutral cure silicone, which does not emit the corrosive acid. More expensive and requiring a longer cure period, this form of single-component silicone is safe to use.

As a sealant, silicone needs at least 23 hours' exposure to air and humidity to cure. As an adhesive, the bonding cure may require a week's exposure to air and humidity. A ⅛- to ¼-inch-diameter bead achieves maximum strength. Thicker layers require more drying time and are weaker. Should any portion of the white PVC piping be exposed to sunlight, perhaps where the pipe leaves the ground to re-enter the water feature system, paint the pipe black. This prevents the plastic from deteriorating and turning brittle and cracking.

Class 200 (thin wall) PVC is available in diameters of ½", ¾", and 1". For larger diameters, use Schedule 40 (thick wall) PVC. Usually the size of the outlet port on the pump is appropriate to the pump's output. Many professionals and pondkeepers feel that adapting the port to the next larger diameter produces a more satisfactory flow, particularly with waterfalls. Likewise, if the tubing is of any significant length, adapting to the next larger diameter produces a

Submersible pumps are usually equipped with a grate or screen over the intake to help prevent solid matter from cycling through the pump. Photo by H. Nash

stronger flow. Eamonn Hughes recommends adapting the size up by ½ inch to 1 inch to reduce friction loss if the delivery hose is longer than 50 feet. A ball valve added near the pump allows control of up to 50 percent of the flow. Check the operating instructions of the pump before your purchase to verify that the pump can handle your desired restriction. If you close the valve to any degree, watch for additional reduction of flow, which indicates trapped debris in the line; relieve the blockage and avoid stressing the pump by opening and closing the valve.

Flexible tubing commonly available in the smaller diameters used

for fountains and piped statuary is often clear plastic. If the tubing is exposed to sunlight, algae quickly builds up inside the tube and decreases the flow. Trying to clean a length of narrow tubing is awkward if not impossible. Rather than replacing the tubing frequently, use black plastic tubing that blocks light and discourages algae growth.

A common means of water delivery in the ½-inch to 1-inch range is a garden hose. A very flexible, reinforced, all-weather hose will usually do the job. Avoid using a hose that may split open in freezing climates.

Eamonn uses a flexible, reinforced spa hose that he finds easy to install. He recommends that flexible hoses be reinforced to

Setting your pump inside a basket makes it easier to retrieve from the pond for cleaning. Photo by H. Nash

Recommended Tubing Diameter for Pumps to Waterfalls

½ inch diameter	for flows up to	120 gph
¾ inch diameter	for flows up to	350
1 inch	for flows up to	1000
1¼ inch	for flows up to	1500
1½ inch	for flows up to	3000 gph

avoid hose-wall collapse and restricted flow. He notes that elbow attachments produce noticeable reductions in flow.

If you decide to have more than one water feature in your water garden, use one pump to feed them all by gluing tees into the delivery line with ball valves on each tee. Adjust the various flows by closing each tee to a different degree.

PUMP MAINTENANCE

How much attention is required by the pump depends on how clean the waters are that it circulates. Water containing suspended particles—soil, organic matter, or algae—deposits this material on the intake port. Collected particulate matter stresses the pump and shortens its life. Submersible bottom-intake pumps with only a grate over the intake and submerged open-port pumps should be supplied with appropriate screen protection. The larger this screen area, the less frequently it needs cleaning. Many pumps come equipped with a mesh screen covering the intake, but often these screen attachments require supplemental screening, such as wrapping the pump within a large piece of stainless steel, fiberglass, or fabric mesh screen.

Early spring and early autumn are generally the periods of highest organic loading in the pond. Check the pump's filter screen often, at least weekly during this time. Shut off the pump and remove it and its filter attachments from the water to hose them clean with a strong jet of water. Replace filter media as needed. With external pumps, check the filter media and screening provisions to clean as necessary.

In shallow waters that serve fountain assemblies or small ponds, remove the pump for the winter if your water freezes. Clean the pump and store it in a non-freezing area. Store the pump containing oil coolant in a bucket of water to prevent the seals from drying, cracking, and producing oil leaks. Magnetic-drive pumps may be stored dry. In areas that freeze, clean and disconnect the centrifugal, external pump. Leave all bottom valves open to drain all water from the unit. Pumps that will be left running through the winter season should be moved up into the upper third of the pond, to avoid cycling colder surface water into the warmer water below where fish are resting for the season. Some pondkeepers disconnect waterfall or fountain connections and allow the pump to bubble at the surface, thereby keeping a hole open in ice formation. Allowing the pump to run waterfalls during heavy ice formations is not advised, since ice buildup can result in hidden water loss.

FILTRATION

Although clear water is a goal for most pondkeepers, it is only part of a filter's work. Even though your water is crystal clear, invisible, fish-toxic chemicals can be present. A good filter will not only remove solid particles and green-water algae, but it will also control fish-toxic chemicals produced in fish wastes and in the normal nitrogen cycle at work in the pond water.

As discussed in Chapter Three, the nitrogen cycle converts organic debris into fish-harmful ammonia and nitrite and finally into harmless nitrate. Filters provide media to collect debris and to provide a home for the beneficial nitrifying bacteria that enhance this naturally occurring process.

Sizing Your Pond's Filter

The size of a filter is determined primarily by the pond's volume and by the type of filter—low-pressure or high-pressure— you will use. Other factors to consider are the pond's site and design, how many and what type of plants and fish are kept in the pond, what and how often the fish are fed, the filter's purpose, the type of media used in it, and the maintenance required.

While the familiar swimming pool filter relies on toxic chemicals such as chlorine and bromine to clean the water, the water garden with its plants and fish cannot do so. Much less particulate matter cycles through swimming pools, too, than in a pond that literally grows its own organic wastes. Effective pond filters, therefore, are much larger than those used for swimming pools. That size presents problems of aesthetics—how to hide it. Cleverly designed, manufactured units that look like waterfalls or planters are large enough to adequately service no more than 300 gallons of pond volume.

Calculating Pond Volume

Before you decide what type of filter to use, you need to figure your pond's volume. The most accurate way to do this, of course, is to meter the water as you fill the pond. If you are planning your filter at the time you are planning your pond construction, however, you must rely on mathematical formulas to determine the size filter to build or use. Factors such as sloping sides, plant shelves, and irregular shapes may prevent precise computations. Use these formulas to approximate pond volume, leaning toward the higher side of the estimate to assure filter effectiveness.

First measure the *average* length, width, and depth of the pond. In an irregularly designed pond, use the maximum width, length, and depth. Convert these measurements into feet. A 30-inch depth, for example, equals 2½ feet, or 2.5 feet. Multiply the length by the width and then multiply that by the depth. Finally, multiply that figure by 7.48 (the number of gallons of water in a cubic foot). If the pond has rounded corners and sides, you can compensate by multiplying the volume figure by 0.85.

For round ponds, convert all measurements into feet, multiply the radius (which is half the diameter) by itself, and then multiply that by 3.14. Multiply that figure by the average depth to determine the pond's volume in cubic feet. Finally, multiply the volume in cubic feet by 7.48 to determine the approximate number of gallons of water in the pool.

$$\text{length} \times \text{width} \times \text{depth} \times 7.48 = \text{gallons per cubic foot}$$
$$\text{for a round pond: } r^2 \times 3.14 \times \text{depth} \times 7.48 = \text{gallons per cubic foot}$$

Don't forget to include the number of gallons of water held in other ponds, waterfalls, and streams included within the recycling system.

Low- and High-Pressure Biomechanical Filters

Armed with the critical information about the volume of water in your pond, you can calculate the size filter needed. Gravity-fed or gravity-return systems rely on movement of water through the system to collect waste products that might cloud the water. Because water movement must be slow enough to allow particle settlement (mechanical filtration) and leave enough time for nitrifying bacteria to work on ammonia and nitrites in the water (biological filtration), these systems are considered low pressure. The total volume of pond water should be recirculated through the filter every three hours and no more often than every 30 minutes. Combining the two functions of mechanical filtration and biological nitrification qualifies such systems as biomechanical.

Low pressure biomechanical filters, which use such media as matting or brushes, should hold 7 to 10 percent of the total volume of water in the pond. This means that an 8 × 10 foot pond with an average depth of 2 feet, and holding approximately 1200 gallons of water, should have 84 to 120 gallons in the filter chamber. With synthetic media, such a system is feasible if the filter chamber is slightly larger than the size of an 80-gallon whiskey barrel container. If less expensive gravel is used as the filter medium, the filter should hold 23 to 28 percent of the pond's total volume. The 8 × 10-foot pond that is 2 feet deep would then require a filter chamber holding 275 to 335 gallons, approximately a 4 × 5 × 2-foot-deep pond. If you heed the advice (and lament) of pond owners and make your pond as large as possible, space to accommodate both pond and filter system becomes a major consideration. However, a 7 to 10 percent filter needs to be cleaned only once

For the very small pond, internal box filters can be attached to your pump.
Photo courtesy of Little Giant Pump Corporation

The filter system should hold 7 to 10 percent of the volume of your pond for most effective service. Photo by H. Nash

or twice a year. Planning ahead to include enough space for an appropriate-size filter ensures yearlong enjoyment of your pond while minimizing the need for maintenance.

But what if your space is at a premium and you don't want to "waste" it with filter setups? It can be done, but will need increased maintenance. Actually, only one percent of the pond volume is required in a biological filter to tend the nitrogen cycle conversions for safe water quality. Such a system must be cleaned several times a week and may never achieve maximum effectiveness with the constant disruption of the bacteria. A 4 to 6 percent filter, on the other hand, requires cleaning every 8 to 12 weeks, depending on your fish

and plant load. Size of the filter system and maintenance become more manageable within this range, though you may sacrifice water clarity and experience chronic or constant bouts of green or cloudy water. A supplemental ultraviolet clarifier unit solves these problems.

Recent developments have produced another option for the space-conscious water gardener—high-pressure filters. These filter designs are based on the compact designs of the high-pressure swimming pool/spa sand filters. Using media known as "buoyant beads," these filters offer maximum area for bacterial colonies within a small space, but the units themselves require camouflage for their tall, unsightly presence. Like traditional swimming pool filter systems, these high-pressure filters require frequent cleaning, often daily. Expensive automatic methods can't end this chore. Many early users of these new systems quickly became disillusioned, because even though the water quality remained safe for the fish,

Wrapping the pump inside layers of filter matting expands the area of mechanical filtration for the pump.
Photo by Oliver Jackson

it was perpetually murky, cloudy, and green. These filters are so efficient, the end product of the nitrogen cycle—nitrates—are produced in such abundance they foster the growth of free-floating, green water algae. Properly stocking nutrient-using submerged grasses may curtail this algae growth. Adding a supplemental UVC filter may ensure clear water. If you do use a UVC, mechanical filtration is necessary to prevent micro-organisms from decomposing in the pond and thereby resulting in another generation of algae bloom.

FILTER OPTIONS

As you consider the type of filter system to use, remember that every pond is different, even from one yard to the next. What works for one pondkeeper may not work at all for you. Even more important, in spite of an enthusiast's claims, there is no one right way. Consider these five basic types of filter options: internal biomechanical filters, external biomechanical filters, external mechanical filters, external biological filters, and other filters.

Internal Biomechanical Filters

Internal Box Filters

Internal filters (submersible filters) are placed inside the pond. Typically a plastic box with a screen at the water intake, these filters use media such as foam, mat, or gravel for biomechanical filtration. The pump may be enclosed within the unit or may be separate but attached to the filter box at the water-intake port. The pump pulls water through the filter box and discharges it through a plumbed water feature, such as a fountain or waterfall. Filter matting is the most effective medium. Foam (sponge) tends to clog quickly, as do gravel-type media.

The problem with these filters is that bacterial or bio-filtration occurs in the same place as the mechanical or particulate filtration. Even if you provide the recommended 7 to 10 percent area of filtration, organic debris collects on the media, and so aerobic nitrifying bacteria can be suffocated. Weekly water tests for ammonia and nitrite indicate if the filter is losing effectiveness and needs cleaning. If your fish load is minimal and you use supplemental filter elements, such as plants (and possibly a UVC), submersible filter boxes can be effective for the small pond (under 300 gallons, or approximately 4 × 5 feet and 2 feet deep.) In a fish-stocked pond with no supplemental filtration, even the largest of these commercially available units cannot fully serve a pond over 100 gallons. Plan on cleaning such units at least once a month.

Under-Gravel Filters

Familiar to aquarium keepers, the under-gravel filter is a shallow tray installed over approximately 20 to 50 percent of the pond bottom. An intake assembly, either a grate or a perforated pipe, is installed on the bottom of the filter tray with a 4- to 10-inch layer of ⅜- to ½-inch rounded gravel placed on top of it. The pump draws water from the bottom of the tray to create a

After the first two years, an under-gravel filter may require a major annual cleaning. Photo by Lee Dreyfuss

downward flow through the gravel bed. The gravel serves as a mechanical filter. It traps organic debris and also serves as a medium for the growth of nitrifying bacteria.

These systems usually require no maintenance at all for the first year or two. After that, clean the gravel annually, usually in the early spring. Such major cleaning involves emptying the pond and siphon-vacuuming accumulated debris from the gravel. Another way is with weekly or biweekly water exchanges of 5 percent of the pond's volume, vacuuming a portion of the gravel bed. If you choose such a maintenance program, monitor your water quality for ammonia and nitrite to make sure the filter continues working effectively through the cleaning period. (See Chapter Seven, Cleaning the Pond.)

The consensus of opinion is that the system works. The one precaution to observe with under-gravel filters is to keep aquatic plants from taking hold in the gravel and impairing the function of the filter. Submerged grasses can take hold quickly in these ideal conditions. Under-gravel filters

installed in depths of 18 inches or less invite vigorous growers, such as water clovers, floating hearts, and bog beans, to take root. Controversy exists over vacuuming: some people contend that pond vacuuming itself is not effective when siphoning a lower elevation (the pond bottom). Our experience has been that it takes time, but it does work. Under-gravel filter systems may be more appropriate for fish ponds than for true aquatic plant gardens.

An adaptation of the under-gravel filter uses synthetic media, such as fiber matting or brushes, instead of gravel. Because the bed can be deeper, less of the pond bottom may be required for the installation. However, the media must be removed from the pond for cleaning (hosing). Removing the media without clouding the water with particulate matter is all but impossible.

External Biomechanical Filters

External biomechanical filters are installed outside the pond. These units may be low pressure, relying on some form of gravity feed or

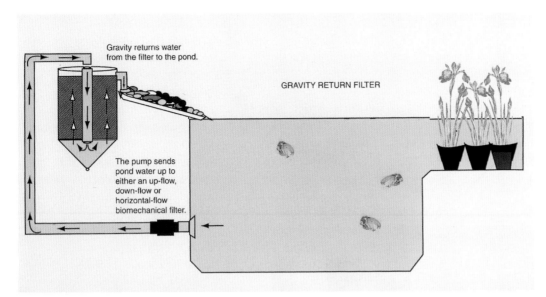

Gravity returns water
from the filter to the pond.

GRAVITY RETURN FILTER

The pump sends
pond water up to
either an up-flow,
down-flow or
horizontal-flow
biomechanical filter.

*Gravity-return biome-
chanical filter*

Drawing courtesy of Santa
Fe Water Gardens, Santa
Fe, New Mexico

return, or they may be high-pressure units similar in operation to
swimming pool/spa sand filters.

Gravity-Return Biomechanical Filter

In this style filter, the pump forces
water into a filter chamber, where it
flows through the media and then
returns to the pond by the force of
gravity. These systems need to be
sited at the highest point in the system, such as at the top of a waterfall or stream course. Of the three
flow designs—up-flow, horizontal-
flow, and down-flow—the up-flow
and horizontal-flow are considered
better. Regardless of the design cho-
sen, it should accommodate 7 to 10
percent of the total pond volume
for maximum effectiveness. These
designs are easily added to existing
ponds if filtration is necessary.

Up-Flow Filters

In an up-flow system, the pump
sends water to the top of the filter,
where it flows down an oxygenating
tower to the bottom of the unit.

There, a disbursement area
created with a grate sup-
ports the filter media above
an open cavity of one to
two inches. Water chan-
neled down the tower exits
into the open cavity,
swirling around and flowing
upward through the media
to overflow through a side
port near the top of the unit
for return to the pond. Solid
wastes are collected in the
bottom cavity and removed
through a bottom drain.
The design also allows the
filter media to be back-
washed. Non-floating media, such
as lava rocks, work well in this
design, although the grate must be
strong enough to support them.

Horizontal-Flow Filters

In the horizontal-flow system,
water is pumped through a side

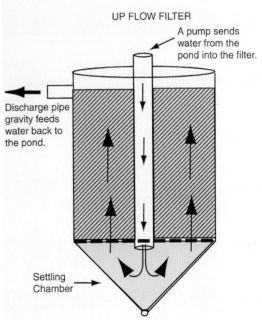

UP FLOW FILTER

A pump sends
water from the
pond into the filter.

Discharge pipe
gravity feeds
water back to
the pond.

Settling
Chamber

wall of the filter unit to flow horizontally through the media and
then exit through a port on the
opposite side. These systems often
include baffling walls to create a
zigzag flow through the chamber,
allowing particles to settle out as
water circulates through the full

area of media. Recommended media for such units are lighter in weight than gravel or lava rock, and include synthetics, such as matting, brushes, open-cell foam, and bio-ribbon. Bottom drains make it easy to remove settled particulates, but backwashing to clean the filter media is not very effective. Instead, drain the unit and gently hose the media inside the chamber or outside, as is appropriate. Bio-ribbon can be stirred by hand while being gently hosed. Tend brushes either inside the chamber or outside, and remove foam for cleaning.

Down-Flow Filters

In a down-flow system, water is pumped to the top of the chamber, where it flows down through the media to exit from the bottom. As solid wastes collect in the upper portion of the medium, the media compacts and reduces the filter's efficiency. Thick-fibered matting is the preferred medium because it is easy to remove and clean. Since

Gravity-fed filter systems pump water to the highest elevation, circulating it through the filter and returning it by gravity back to the reservoir pond. Photo by H. Nash

backwashing is not an effective cleaning method, this system is the most labor-intensive of the three to maintain.

Gravity-Fed Biomechanical Filters

Gravity-fed biomechanical filters use one or more chambers at or below water level and are fed by a feed pipe either from the side wall of the pond or from a bottom drain. These chambers are easily concealed in the floor of the decking or in the ground. For flows up to 5000 GPH, the feed pipes should be 3 to 6 inches in diameter. Feed pipes should avoid elbow joints that encourage clogging.

Another method is to have water overflow from the pond into a stream that carries the water to the filter before it returns to the pond. Be sure the chambers are large enough to handle the volume of water for the entire out-of-pond portion of the system when the system is shut down.

As noted previously, up-flow and horizontal-flow designs are preferred, and synthetic media are less prone to compaction. Because of the intrusion of the feed pipe through either the side wall of the pond or through a bottom drain, retrofitting an existing pond with such systems can be challenging and expensive.

Buoyant-Bead Filters

Rather than collecting waste in the filter chamber and breaking it down biologically, buoyant bead filters collect waste and discharge it from the pond system before decomposition begins. Less expen-

sive models require the pond owner to backwash the system as frequently as once or more daily. Operating on the one-percent-media formula primarily to service the biological filtration needs of the pond, these filters appear quite large, as they often may be taller than a person. Camouflaging them behind a tall screen or within a nearby building is necessary for aesthetics.

Buoyant-bead filters are up-flow filters. Nontoxic polyethylene beads are the filter media. As water is pumped into the bottom of the filter chamber, the beads float to the top and compress slightly to create a biomechanical filter bed. "Bubble bead" filters are cleaned by turning off the pump and opening

The new buoyant-bead filters operate on a one-percent-of-pond-volume formula, to maximize bio-filtration and to discharge organic debris before it has a chance to decompose. Photo by H. Nash

the drain valve in the bottom. As the water leaves the chamber, air is drawn inside and air bubbles agitate the media, dislodging trapped solids and discharging them out the bottom. Turning the pump back on restores normal operation. Other systems clean beads very effectively with a pressurized jet of water. Some large buoyant-bead filters designed for ponds of 20,000 or more gallons are equipped with a built-in, motorized, cleaning propeller.

The pressurized discharge of returning the water to the pond allows the filter to be used in stream and waterfall return systems from as much as 400 or 500 feet from the pond. The most successful use of these systems to maintain both clear and fish-safe water is in conjunction with a UV clarifier.

Recent adaptations of the buoyant-bead filter include fluidized bed technology, which uses a smaller sized bead. The smaller bead "polishes" the water for greater water clarity. Such a system requires a high-pressure-tolerant pump, which uses more electricity. The big advantage of this type of system is its ability to carry larger fish loads in the pond safely.

External Biological Filters

Out-of-pond or external bio-filters allow accessibility and easier maintenance while keeping particulate collection separate from bio-filtration. This helps preserve the life of bacteria by preventing suffocation by accumulated matter.

The most commonly used medium for bio-filters has been lava rock. However, lava rock accumulates particulates. Cleaning rock media can be difficult and time-consuming; although if the filter is the proper size for the pond, the medium may need cleaning only two or three times through the entire pond season.

In recent years, other efficient media have been developed. Lushly dense poly brushes are one type. Another recent introduction is bio-ribbon, simply long, narrow strips of poly material. Some pond owners have found that compressing poly bird-netting is an inexpensive option. These types of media provide adequate surface area and are stirred by hand for a quick cleaning. Such media are especially useful to the pond owner who builds a filter.

For the pond owner who wishes to buy an effective external bio-filter, fluidized bed filters offer the maximum surface area for bacteria. Very fine silica sand that normally sinks in water is suspended by an upward-flowing column of water. With the flow rate set to prevent the sand from being blown out of the filter or from settling to the bottom, bacteria can grow on as much as 5000 square feet of surface area per cubic foot of media. Channeling that would occur in stable sand beds is avoided because each grain is in constant motion.

EXTERNAL MECHANICAL FILTERS

Purely mechanical filters are designed for efficient solid waste collection with little, if any, biological action. *High-pressure sand filters,* the typical swimming pool/spa unit, force water through a densely packed bed of sand that is usually housed in a fiberglass, stainless steel, or plastic chamber. Similarly, *cartridge filters* force water through densely woven, pleated cartridges housed in cylindrical stainless steel or plastic chambers. Both filters tend to be high maintenance, but don't use pond-toxic chlorine, hydrogen peroxide, or bromine. These styles are so maintenance intensive, they are impractical for pondkeeping.

Settling tanks are simply big

High-pressure sand filters, used in swimming pools and at spas, are a high-maintenance option even when part of the sand is replaced with larger media.
Photo by Al Savaikis

tanks of water that allow debris to settle to the bottom. The water velocity is slowed so particulates in the water fall out of suspension and settle to the bottom of the tank. Most settling tanks have a conical bottom that concentrates the debris in a small area for easy removal by flushing out a bottom drain. This wastes less water than

Settling tanks can be installed as the first stage or two of a complete biomechanical filter system. Photo by Phil Alexander

OTHER FILTER OPTIONS
Ultraviolet Clarifiers

Ultraviolet clarifiers (UV's or UVC's) are the easiest and most space-efficient way to achieve reliable water clarity. A cylindrical chamber houses an ultraviolet lightbulb, which is protected by a clear quartz sleeve. Water is pumped into the filter and exposed to high-intensity ultraviolet light that kills living organisms suspended in the water. While koi hobbyists often use UV filter units to kill disease organisms, the units are now used most often to control planktonic algae that cause cloudy, green water. What is killed and at what rate depend on the intensity and duration of exposure. Most pond-grade systems are set for minimal intensity and exposure time to remove free-floating algae. UVC's do not substitute for the biological activity of biofilters. While UVC units kill water-borne organisms, they do not remove them or the by-products produced by their decomposition in water. A good mechanical filter or appropriate vacuuming removes particulate matter, and a biological filter converts ammonia

Ultraviolet clarifiers use ultraviolet light to kill microscopic organisms, including planktonic algae. Photo by Oliver Jackson

produced in decomposition to its eventual non-toxic nitrates.

While it can take these units up to two weeks to clear the water in larger ponds, water is often clear in small ponds in a few days. Because of the expense of operating the lights, many pondkeepers run them only when the water begins to be cloudy. The lightbulbs should be replaced annually.

Chemical Filtration

Chemical filtration for ponds simply means using carbon to adsorb compounds dissolved on its surface and zeolite to chemically absorb ammonia from the water. Although carbon can be rinsed and reused and zeolite can be recharged by soaking it overnight in a solution of one pound of non-iodized salt dissolved in five gallons of water, carbon and zeolite are both generally too expensive and impractical to use as the only form of filtration. They work well for emergency or short-term situations, however.

flat-bottom tanks. Settling tanks are normally installed before, and used in conjunction with, either gravity-fed or gravity-return filter chambers. The most efficient settling tanks are round with side ports for water injection, so entering water engages in a circular or vortex flow that aids settlement. Such settling tanks are commonly used as the first and sometimes first and second chambers of an external filtration system, the biological chamber being the final stop for the water before it returns to the pond.

Diagram of Phil Alexander's filter system, using two settling chambers (left) *and one biofiltration chamber* (right). Drawing by Phil Alexander

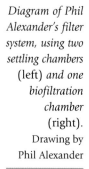

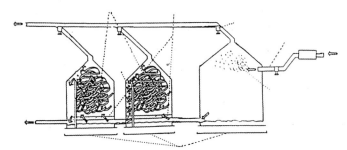

Phyto-Filtration or Vegetative/Plant Filtration

For the pond under-stocked with fish, vegetative filtration may be all that is needed to maintain both water quality and clarity. For maximum effectiveness, the vegetative filter should be set up as a separate pond equal to 10 to 20 percent of the surface area of the main pond. At 12 to 18 inches in depth, this pond can accommodate both submerged aquatic plants that remove excess nutrients from the water along with marginal or shallow-water aquatics that aid in nutrient removal and particle settlement (and use of that settlement as food).

Obviously, the water must move slowly enough through the plant filter area to allow particle settlement, usually no more rapidly than circulating the pond volume every two to four hours. While the plants can be potted, they can also be grown in gravel and in gravel-topped, soil-filled planting pockets within the vegetative filter pond. Growing plants in a slow-moving stream bed accomplishes the same end, although you must watch that plants do not fill the stream and cause flooding and water loss.

Controlling the growth of planktonic or green water algae usually requires at least one bunch of submerged plants per square foot or two of water surface and perhaps as much as 60 percent of the water surface covered by floating leaves/plants to shade the water.

An adaptation of vegetative filtration is to grow plants in mesh containers with their roots fully

Special preformed units can be fit into your pond system to supply vegetative filtration.
Photo by Bob Romar, courtesy of Maryland Aquatic Nurseries

Double-pond construction allows the upper pond to be used as a vegetative filter.
Photo by H. Nash

exposed to the water. However, plants that traditionally grow in soil may not receive enough nutrients in water. Do not be afraid to experiment with plants to test their suitability to your purpose. Remember that even aquatic plants, whether submersed, emergent, or floating, perform photosynthesis during the daylight hours and produce oxygen as a by-product. During the nighttime hours, the plants perform respiration, using oxygen to produce carbon dioxide as a by-product. If your fish population begins to approach a maximum stocking level, test your water regularly to be sure ammonia and

nitrite are not becoming problems that must be dealt with by supplemental biological filtration. As long as your fish population is kept under control, vegetative filtration alone can be sufficient.

Slow-moving streams can also be planted as vegetative filters. Monitor sediment buildup to prevent the water level from rising and flooding. Photo by H. Nash

CHAPTER SEVEN

Solving Problems

ALGAE

Murky green water, slimy filamentous strands wrapped around your plants, and fuzzy, hairy green strands affixed to the pond or to the sides of the pot are all forms of pond algae. All are a form of plant life, a lower form than those purposely grown in gardens. The fuzzy stuff on the sides of pots acts much like the submerged grasses grown in ponds to help remove excess nitrates. Aesthetically, this mossy growth naturalizes the wet surfaces within the garden by camouflaging them. If you feel compelled to remove this growth, a simple scrubbing with a brush does the trick. Filamentous algae are also known as blanket weed. Ironically, these algae do not occur in the presence of the more common pea-soup algae. Seen under a microscope, filamentous algae grow in long, hairlike strands. Wrapped around tender young growth, they can strangle and kill plants. Heavy concentrations can also suffocate plants or deprive them of necessary sunlight. Like other algae, filamentous algae can enter the pond by the air and wind.

Often they enter the pond on plants introduced into the pond. To prevent this, rinse and clean all new plants with salt water at a rate of six tablespoons per gallon of water. Swish plants and expose all

Learning the Language

aeration device—a means of adding additional oxygen to water; in hospital tank use, usually an air pump fitted with an air stone

algae—a simple plant form that proliferates in water in the presence of nutrients and sunlight

ammonia detoxifier—a chemical product that reduces toxic ammonia (NO_3) by causing an extra oxygen atom to bond to the molecule and form a non-toxic ammonia (NO_4)

anaerobic activity—the process of decomposing organic matter without the presence of oxygen by anaerobic bacteria, producing fish-toxic gases as by-products

hibernation—in fish, a period during low-water temperatures in which the fish's metabolism slows significantly and the fish lives off its stored body fat

filamentous algae—slimy, stranded algae, also known as blanket weed

flashing—fish behavior in which the fish quickly sideswipes a pot or the pond wall to scratch an irritation on its skin

flocculent—commercially available chemicals that cause particles such as single-celled algae to clump together for easier removal

mother rhizome—the parent plant that produces additional growing points either along or within the rhizome

mulm—very fine particulate matter that collects on the pond bottom

phyto-filtration—use of plants, especially submerged grasses, to remove excess nutrients from the water and thereby prevent algae growth

pond vac—a cleaning method to remove particulate matter from the pond bottom, usually based on siphon principles

quarantine tank—usually, a glass aquarium tank set up to treat sick fish or to observe new ones to verify their health before addition to the pond

stress—in fish, a condition caused by overcrowding, transportation, parasites, or disease, resulting in a fish losing its protective slime coating and becoming vulnerable to parasitic attack or disease

tannic acid—acid released into water by pine needles and oak and maple leaves; turns water a brownish cast and, in sufficient quantity, jeopardizes fish

water dye—dye, usually black or blue, that shades water and thereby hinders algae growth

Filamentous algae, also known as blanket weed, can literally choke your plants to death.   Photo by Ron Everhart

Green water results when sunlight and excess nutrients in water feed single-celled, free-floating microscopic algae plants. Photo by Bill Marocco

able in the U.S. Known as Pond Balance, the pink crystals are dissolved in water and added to the pond in the early spring. Testing has shown it to be effective in controlling blanket weed, but stubborn cases may require regular applications throughout the season. While the company does not label the package with ingredients, it states the product is not a chemical like copper sulfate.

The easiest way to control filamentous algae may be with water dyes. These provide microscopic particles in black or blue that fracture light and prevent it from penetrating into the water, thereby preventing the growth of blanket weed algae. The dyes dissipate in time, so reapplication during the season may be necessary. If you use dyes early in the season before your aquatic plants have resumed seasonal growth, move the dormant plants close to the water surface to allow sunlight to reach them.

The most common form of algae in water gardens is the pea-soup form of free-floating, single-celled green plant. This form is often found in the early spring

Many botanical gardens use water dye to shade water and prevent the growth of green-water algae.   Photo by H. Nash

before plants have begun to grow. Fortunately, this nemesis can be controlled. Algae, like other plants, need sunlight and nutrients. Sixty percent of surface coverage is often suggested as a remedy because it produces the requisite shade for the pond water. However, in zones colder than tropical zone 10, the early spring is too soon to add floating plants such as water hyacinth, so very few water gardeners in the United States can resort to this technique. Similarly, water

surfaces to the salt solution, then rinse the plants well before placing them in the pond. Twirling a stick or a bottle brush in the water will remove most of this offensive plant. A product produced by Interpet in England is now avail-

As long as your fish population is under control, submerged grasses will usually keep the water clear. Photo by H. Nash

lilies have not resumed enough growth at the early time of spring algae bloom.

Many botanical gardens use dyes to color water either blue or black to shade water and prevent this type of algae growth. This is not only effective, it also makes for an attractive and deep-looking pond. However, shading provided by the dye also shades potted aquatics about to resume seasonal growth. Move water lilies and submerged grasses very close to the surface of the water to benefit from needed sunlight and to avoid stunted growth or death.

Vegetative filters that make use of submerged, floating, and marginal plants can remove algae-feeding nutrients from the water. Photo by H. Nash

We are fortunate that in our zone 5 climate the submerged grass *Elodea canadensis* breaks dormancy at about the same time as normally occurring spring algae bloom. By supplying our ponds with at least one bunch of this grass per square foot of water surface, we have completely avoided episodes of green water. The principle behind the use of submerged grasses to access water nutrients before the lower plant form of free-floating algae

UVC clarifiers can kill free-floating algae. Remove dead plants from the water before they decompose and foster another green-water episode.
Photo by Oliver Jackson

can do so is phyto-filtration or vegetative filtration.

It should be mentioned, though, that we are careful with the stocking level of fish and do not feed the fish excessively. We leave in the pond only what the fish will eat in 5 to 10 minutes to prevent excess food from joining in the nitrogen cycle.

Many pondkeepers supply vegetative filtration units or areas within their pond system to achieve such nutrient intervention. Richard Schuck of Maryland Aquatic Nurseries came up with a formula for this type of natural filtration many years ago. He called it the "Ten Percent Solution." Essentially, he learned from experience that green-water algae did not occur

when he supplied a flow-through area of submerged and marginal aquatic plants equal to 10 percent of the pond's surface area. Many pondkeepers have discovered that such an area can be supplied in a double-pond system in which the upper-level pond is from 10 to 20 percent the size of the lower pond. The upper pond is then stocked with a variety of submerged and marginal plants with the water moving slowly through that pond and into the lower reservoir pond, so particulate matter also settles out of the water. This method of natural filtration is fully effective at achieving both clear and healthy water so long as your fish population is kept within bounds.

One method of clearing water in ponds that are heavily stocked with fish or in which fish are fed well is to use an ultraviolet clarifier. Free-floating algae that move beneath the UV lamp are killed and water is cleared within several days. Using a flocculent or coagulant to clump the dying microscopic plants aids in their removal before they can begin decomposing and fueling another bloom. Mechanical filtration, pond vacuuming, or netting

Pond vacs are one way to remove killed and sedimented algae from the pond bottom. Photo by Oliver Jackson

with a fine-mesh swimming-pool skimmer can also remove them. It is not necessary to run the lamp full-time during the season. Many pondkeepers use it only when the water appears cloudy and at the beginning of a green-water cycle.

In our *Pond & Garden* magazine, Clair Henley reported a method used in England. Cut holes in half the bottom of a plastic trash container. Fill it half full with old clothing, bulkier and coarser fabrics on top and finer ones and pantyhose on the bottom. Reroute the submerged pump to cycle water through the container set on the pond edge, allowing water to return to the pond. After an hour or two, disconnect the device, roll away the container, and hose out the clothing. Repeat as often as necessary until the water is clear. The British use this method against spring algae bloom until plants can begin depriving the algae of nutrients.

AQUATIC INSECTS

Fortunately, the water garden is relatively free of insect pests. Those lovely dragonflies and damselflies, which regularly patrol our summer garden, eat many of the pests that might otherwise present problems. Pests that might visit your garden and create unsightly havoc are few: aphids, moths, and midges.

Although many gardeners profess that aphids are attracted to dying leaves (keep them pruned away as they start to yellow) or by otherwise diseased or disfigured leaves, aphids also appear on perfectly healthy plants. The most

commonly offered solution for water-garden aphids is to hose them into the water for the fish to eat. In practice, aphids are quicker at scrambling back on board than fish are at feasting on them. Because you don't want to use any chemical insecticides in your pond that might harm your fish, the safest remedy may be mixing vegetable oil and water (with a splash of dishwashing detergent to emulsify the oil) and spraying it onto the pesky critters. The oily film disrupts gas exchanges, so sop away excess oil with paper towels or special oil soakers. (Treat serious infestations chemically in a separate treatment tub, rinsing plants well before returning them to the pond.) Treat nearby fruit trees where aphids winter over with a horticultural oil spray.

Both moths and beetles may lay their eggs in the pond. Their larvae may feed upon aquatic plants, particularly water lily leaves, and seriously disfigure them. Removing infested leaves immediately prevents major problems. "Sandwich man" moth larvae wrap themselves in the protective shelter of floating pieces of leaves

Dragonflies delight the eye and help control flying insect populations.
Photo by Ron Everhart

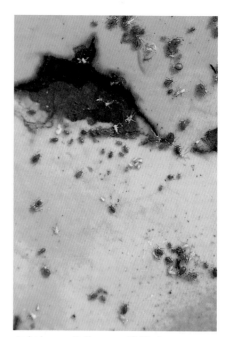
Aphids can disfigure and kill plants.
Photo by Ron Everhart

or debris and feed upon water-lily leaves. They can easily be scooped from the pond. Occasionally, these grublike creatures will be seen using a piece of leaf for the top shelter and the lily leaf itself as the bottom. This is especially noticeable near the leaf petiole, where the leaf attaches to the stem. The larvae work their way to the stem and burrow down, sometimes to the plant rhizome, to pupate. Other grublike larvae roll themselves in the edges of aquatic plants like lotuses. Handpicking usually keeps them under control. Caterpillars and grub larvae can be killed, however, with Bt (*Bacillus thuringiensis*) products, commonly available at garden centers. These products contain otherwise harmless bacteria that parasitize the digestive systems of caterpillars and grub larvae, thereby causing death. You may find that floating mosquito dunks, which are nothing more than a time-release way to get *Bt* into the pond water, are effective in controlling both caterpillars and mosquitoes. Not much research has been done on this means of controlling larval moths and beetles, but since it is not harmful to fish, it might prove a worthwhile experiment. In severe

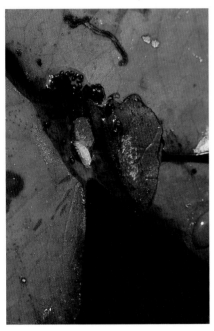

The famous "sandwich man" is a moth grub that hides between pieces of leaves as he feeds on plants.   Photo by H. Nash

infestations, you can safely remove all floating leaves from any one water-lily plant because fresh leaves are quickly produced.

Midges look like swarms of mosquitoes hovering over the pond's surface in the early evening. Their larvae are quite small and burrow

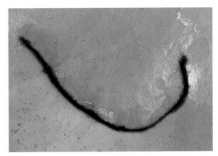

Aquatic midges, like terrestrial leaf miners, burrow disfiguring paths across lily leaves. Photo by Ron Everhart

within the surface tissue of your aquatic plants, especially water-lily leaves. Their damage looks much like that of the terrestrial leaf miner except that in water lilies, the traceries left by the burrowing rot clear through the leaves. *Bt* does not control midges since they are protected within their burrows. Removing affected leaves is the best remedy.

Encouraging dragonflies and damselflies to stay in the yard helps control many flying insect pests in the garden. Removing dying vegetation from the pond regularly also discourages serious attacks. Because insects are part of the pond ecosystem, their larvae providing fish food, a sterile pond is not advisable. The idea is simply to keep the insects under control so they don't overtake the garden.

Many books and mail-order aquatic plant catalogs recommend stocking your pond with "scavengers"—snails. Certain types of snails, such as the ramshorn and the trapdoor, are particularly recommended as not being harmful to your plants. The tall, pointed Great Pond Snail is discouraged because it is an aggressive eater of

aquatic plants. We once found a uniquely scallop-leafed water lily that we excitedly thought to be a wonderful mutation...until we discovered a Great Pond Snail eating its way around the leaf perimeters. Another large-growing snail, the apple snail or mystery snail, is often recommended, too. This breed is tropical and must be wintered indoors in aquariums.

Determine the type of snail present in the pond by looking at the eggs. Ramshorn snails lay eggs in rounded patches of jelly on the undersides of lily leaves. Trapdoor snails are live bearers. Apple snails leave the water and deposit masses of rosy-red eggs on emergent plant stems. The undesirable great pond snail lays its eggs in an extended, often slightly curving, jellylike mass. Use a soft cloth or paper towel to wipe away the eggs before they can hatch. While you can try floating lettuce, cabbage, or Styrofoam sheets in the pond overnight to attract undesirable snails for removal, once they are present, simply keeping a skimmer net handy is the best, albeit tedious, way of ridding the pond of them.

The three snails most commonly found in the water garden: the ramshorn, the trapdoor, and the undesirable Great Pond Snail.   Photo by Ron Everhart

The apple snail grows quite large and must be wintered indoors.
Photo by H. Nash

Carefully check all new plants and rinse them well before adding them to the pond, to prevent accidental introduction of unwanted snails.

The apple snail climbs aerial stems to lay its rosy-red eggs.   Photo by Ron Everhart

Deciding whether to include snails in the pond is a personal decision. After many years we decided not to introduce them deliberately, since they serve as the intermediary host for anchor worms in fish. However, as the saying goes, "If you build it, they will come." We are constantly netting out the unwanted Great Pond Snails, and we are fortunate that our golden retrievers are epicureans at heart and aid in our efforts to eliminate this pest.

FROGS AND TOADS

Frogs and toads and their nymph form, tadpoles, are part of the fascination of pondkeeping. In the early spring and early summer, their breeding lights the night with a melody and cacophony of calls. Even the urban backyard is likely to have tree frogs and toads that will breed in the pond. The tadpoles change into adults within the season, leave the water, and live in the backyard, where they eat many insects.

If you live near a body of water, you may find green frogs, bull frogs, and leopard frogs claiming your pond as home. These larger frogs produce tadpoles that require two seasons to change into frogs. To assure their survival through the winter, provide them with a pot or two of mud in the bottom of your pond. Frogs and tadpoles bury themselves in mud for the winter. Another reason not to scrub away that fuzzy pondside algae is that baby tadpoles feed on it. They will also feed on filamentous algae.

Be very cautious about purchasing tadpoles for your pond. Bullfrog tadpoles are commonly available. If these large frogs escape into the natural environment, they can disrupt the existing ecosystem. A common complaint among pondkeepers is that the frogs move on. Although many people suggest this

Frogs will visit your pond and stay as long as there is food (small fish) to eat.
Photo by Ron Everhart

is because the frogs are looking for mates, most likely they have exhausted the food supply within your pond. One of their favorite foods is baby fish. A large bullfrog or green frog will eat small fish of 2 to 4 inches in length. As part of the natural order of the food chain, frogs help control a pond's fish load. However, when we realized we had a rapidly disappearing hatch of special comet goldfish, we hastily netted these fish and kept them indoors for a year.

PREDATORS

Raccoons are probably the number-one predator pest noted by water gardeners. These adorable-looking creatures are nocturnal feeders that

Toads will breed in your pond and inhabit your garden as insect sentries during their adult life.   Photo by Ron Everhart

The Great Blue Heron is reputedly a solitary feeder, but during its nesting season may feed with a friend.
Photo by Ron Everhart

relish protein (fish) in their diet. In attempting to capture a meal, they can destroy your plants, too. Low-voltage electric wire strung around the pond's perimeter may discourage them, as might fox urine soaked in tampons suspended every few feet around the pond. Having a dog also helps. Most people, however, report the best control is the use of live traps and moving the animals somewhere else.

Herons are another common predator of pond fish. These large birds, sometimes several feet tall, can wipe out a fish population in short order. They feed during both day and night hours. During the breeding season, when the herons feed only within a set distance from their rookery nests, they will feed in twos or threes. (Using a heron statue decoy at this time advertises the availability of food and invites the herons to the feast. During the autumn and winter, however, decoys are effective deterrents.) Herons are also capable of landing within the shallows of your pond, rather than always walking to the water as is commonly reported. (Stringing up low fencing around the pond then proves ineffective.)

A new method of deterring these fish-eating predators from your pond is the motion-sensor sprinkler. Being fairly intelligent birds, many herons make the connection that it is only water squirting at them, so the sprinkler is then little use. Scarecrows and loud radio music, too, may offer temporary protection. In any case, move the device around every day or so to keep the herons unfamiliar with the strategy.

The one sure way to protect your fish from herons is with black plastic predator netting. String the netting above the pond so it doesn't hang into the water where it might trap fish and frogs. Black netting is inconspicuous and can be easily removed.

WATER LOSS AND LEAKS

Be familiar with the normal rate of evaporation in your pond. If you notice a significantly greater loss, you may have a leak. If your pond incorporates a waterfall, turn off the pump and see if the water loss stops. If it does, the leak is within the waterfall system. If the loss continues, allow the pond to rest a few days until the loss stabilizes to normal evaporative loss. Your leak will

Raccoons may be adorable to look at, but they relish your fish.   Photo by Ron Everhart

Inconspicuous black plastic netting may be the only sure way to keep herons out of your pond.   Photo by H. Nash

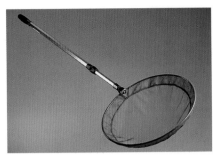

Skimmer nets can be used to scoop decomposing organic matter from the pond bottom.
Photo courtesy of Tetra Second Nature

be at that level. Take a squeeze bottle, fill it with milk, squirt a bit into the water near the pond edge, and watch for the point at which the milk finds the hole. You can then lower the pond below the leak and apply a patch or repair according to the repair kit's directions.

CLEANING THE POND

Normal cleaning through the growing season is simply a matter of scooping out any floating debris and removing dying vegetation and spent blossoms. Mulm or particulate settlement occurs on the pond bottom. This will be a combination of fish waste and other organic and inorganic particles in the water. As long as this layer does not accumulate to more than an inch or so, anaerobic activity that produces fish-toxic hydrogen sulfide and methane gases is not likely to occur. Many pondkeepers regularly vacuum away this mulm with a pond vac that works on a siphon principle. A pond vac may be used

weekly or every few weeks in conjunction with a partial water exchange. Up to 25 percent of the pond water can be replaced with chlorinated water without treatment concerns.

Because pond vacs work by sucking up debris along with water, it is necessary to provide an acceptable drainage acceptor, such as a flower bed or "damp" garden to grow moisture-loving plants. If the siphon unit is attached to the hose outlet of the house, be prepared for a flooded area: Water pulled through the siphon by the flow of water from the spigot will create a puddle.

Even as a heavily fish-loaded pond will benefit from such regular water exchanges, remember that

As plant leaves age, prune and remove them from the garden to prevent them from decomposing in the water.
Photo by H. Nash

cleaning the pond bottom will most likely remove dragonfly nymphs and other small creatures that help establish a natural ecosystem within the pond.

LEAF-FALL

A pond located near shrubs and trees or downwind of them is a leaf catcher in autumn. I remember one autumn when I diligently scooped leaves from a pond every couple hours from dawn until dusk. Several weeks later I was surprised to find many of my small comets floating belly up. Dipping a skimmer net into the pond, I discovered a hefty layer of decomposing leaves! Yes, leaves continue to fall at night! Protect the pond with netting (that wonderful black-plastic predator netting!) or use a swimming pool skimmer net to dip down into the pond and remove the bulk of these leaves. Some leaves, such as maple and oak leaves and pine needles, leach tannic acid, giving the water a distinctly brown cast. This can be deadly to fish, especially in the small water garden.

Pre-Winter Checklist

1. Keep leaves from collecting in the pond.
2. Prepare fish for winter by switching to high-carbohydrate foods (wheat germ-based).

Winterizing Checklist

1. Lower the pond by one-third to tend plants and clean out bottom debris more easily. Treat new water for chlorine if necessary. This fresh water before winter ensures good water quality for hibernating fish.
2. Prune water lilies to within an inch of the crown. Place pots in the deepest portion of the pond where they will not freeze. If your pond might freeze even there, place pot-

The best thing to do with your pond in the winter is to let it rest.
Photo by H. Nash

ted lilies in plastic bags and store in a cool, non-freezing place at 40 to 50 degrees Fahrenheit. Check them during the winter to make sure that they do not fully dry out.
3. Allow one or two hard freezes before removing tropical water lilies. This hardens off their tubers. Hose away soil and free small tubers from the mother plant. Night blooming tropicals have baby tubers embedded within the mother rhizome. Place tubers in plastic bags of damp but not wet white sand and store at 40 to 50 degrees Fahrenheit in a dark place. Check periodically for rot. Tubers may also be air dried for a few hours and then stored in a glass jar of distilled water at the same low temperatures. Fifty degrees is considered ideal.
4. Look to nature for guidance in wintering other aquatic plants. Plants that survive in the wild in your area can be left in place in the pond. Borderline-hardy plants can be buried to their pot rims in the garden and mulched heavily. (Cardinal flower, *Lobelia cardinalis*, is such a plant.) Plants may be pruned in the fall or spring. If pruned in the fall, cut them back

Use the pump set at the pond's surface to keep a hole open in the ice.
Photo by Ron Everhart

Tropical marginal plants can usually be wintered indoors with supplemental lighting. Set the plant pots in deep saucers of water and cut back on fertilizing.
Photo by Oliver Jackson

Plastic tents create mini-greenhouses over small ponds. Photo by Ron Everhart

above the water line to prevent water from rotting the roots. Prune plants such as pickerel that turn mushy in winter.
5. Bring in tropical marginal plants such as umbrella palm before the

first frost. Treat them as house plants, setting them in a deep saucer of water in a sunny window. If plants begin to yellow, supplement window light with 4 to 6 hours of supplemental grow-lights to extend their days. Do not fertilize over the winter.

6. Winter samples of *Azolla* and *Salvinia* in a well-lighted aquarium. Do not place water hyacinths or water lettuce in filtered aquariums, as their fine roots clog the filters. Hyacinths winter indoors more easily than water lettuce. Provide 12 to 14 hours of light and supply liquid fertilizer to the water.

7. Disconnect plumbing to waterfalls and fountains. Clean filters and pumps and store properly. The submerged pump can be set up to bubble at the surface to keep a hole open in ice formations.

8. Any pumps or supplemental aeration provided to the winter pond should be set up in the top third of the pond to avoid cycling colder water into warmer water below where fish are hibernating.

9. Do not run waterfalls during times of heavy ice formations. Water losses can occur.

10. Do not break ice that forms on the pond surface. Doing so can cause concussions in the fish below. Keeping a hole open is advisable, particularly if the pond has not been cleaned of bottom debris that might generate fish-toxic gases. Floating pond heaters can be used, if desired. Plastic tents can be erected over the pond. Slope the tents to facilitate snow removal.

Tropical Pond Checklist

1. Clean the pond as necessary.

2. Switch fish to high-carbohydrate, wheat germ-based foods if water temperature drops to 50 degrees Fahrenheit or below.

3. Hardy water lilies will go dormant. Winter as above or simply leave in place until repotting time in the spring when new growth resumes.

4. Stop fertilizing tropical water lilies and tropical marginal plants to allow a brief rest period.

5. If frost is expected, move tropical water lilies indoors into holding tubs or erect a temporary plastic tent over the pond. Remove the tent during the day to prevent temperatures from building up too high.

GOLDFISH IN WINTER

The depths of winter cloak the pond—snow, ice, or merely chilled waters. Goldfish hover near the pond bottom, motionless, perhaps ringed around a submerged stock heater like campers around an autumn bonfire.

Goldfish come from temperate climates and, although adapted over the years to a wide range of temperatures, still require a hibernation period. The proper hibernation range is 32 to 45 degrees Fahrenheit. Just short of frozen water, this is the range found in the unfrozen depths of the temperate water garden. At these cold temperatures, the fish's metabolism slows to a point of minimal activity. The digestive tract also slows so that

food ingested under these conditions may not be properly digested and may even rot within the fish.

Goldfish are prepared for this period in the autumn by switching them from their high-energy, high-protein summer foods to fat-building, high-carbohydrate foods such as wheat germ-based pellets. They will make it through the winter by using that stored body fat.

Unlike other animals who truly sleep away the winter, goldfish may move lazily about, perhaps cruising the surface on warmer days. Do not be tempted to feed them. They will nibble on submerged grasses if necessary, but their bodies still require six to eight weeks of "hibernation" to ensure their best continued health. Disturb them as little as possible during this period, but observe them for signs of disease or swimming difficulties. Their immune systems are not functioning at this time. Fortunately, parasites that might plague them are also in hibernation mode. If you must remove a fish to a hospital

Even if you winter your goldfish indoors, give them a rest period of light feedings and reduced light.
Photo courtesy of Blue Ridge Fish Hatchery

tank indoors, allow water temperatures to equalize slowly to avoid shocking the fish any further.

If you choose to winter your goldfish indoors, remember the hibernation mode. Keep their tank in a cool location, and reduce feeding and available light to provide a quiet time for 6 to 8 weeks. Many pondkeepers winter the smallest fish indoors.

As long as the pond has been cleaned of excess bottom debris and is not maximally stocked with fish, it does not need additional aeration during the winter. Cold water holds more oxygen than the warm waters of summer. If you do supply aeration, supply it either at the surface by running the submerged pump there or by running an air pump affixed with a long bar airstone kept within the top one-third of the pond water. Keeping a hole open in the ice allows gas exchanges, which is important if decomposition occurs and produces fish-toxic gases. Be sure to protect the air pump from weather.

Ammonia levels are not likely to rise during the winter months because fish metabolism is slow. Monitor ammonia levels in the early spring. Should they rise, execute a partial water exchange of no more than 25 percent of the total pond volume, and take advantage of the chore to perform your spring opening.

Goldfish are a hardy breed of fish, and hibernation is part of their life cycle. Given a clean, quiet bed in which to sleep, they awaken in spring ready to resume their active lives.

SETTING UP A QUARANTINE/ HOSPITAL/INDOOR FISH TANK

Any new fish added to your pond should be closely observed for two full weeks. Always assume a new fish is infected with parasites. Be especially cautious of adding "feeder" goldfish to the pool. Since these fish are bred to be part of the food chain, less care may have been taken to ensure their good health. If the new fish are the only ones in the pool, the entire pool may be treated. Otherwise, it is less expensive, as well as more manageable, to treat a new fish in a smaller, more observable tank such as a glass aquarium.

A glass aquarium may be set up as a hospital tank. It should be equipped with at least an aeration device, usually an air pump with an airstone attached. A recirculating filter may also be used, but should be equipped with only ammonia-absorbing media and filter floss or foam. Activated charcoal will immediately filter any medications from the water. Since many medications also require vigorous aeration, the air pump may still be required with the presence of an aquarium filter. To determine the fish-holding capacity of the aquarium, compute the square surface area of the tank in inches. Divide this figure by 30 to determine the number of body inches the tank can accommodate. Since overcrowding is also stressful, it is important not to add this factor to an already stressed and sick fish.

New fish should be treated with a broad-spectrum parasite medication. Antibiotics should not be used unless a specific disease is noticed. One or two tablespoons of salt per five gallons of water assists in relieving stress as well as in treating parasites. If medications are not available, the 5 g/l dosage for the two-week period may suffice.

The water temperature in a hospital tank should be maintained at a stable level close to that of the pool. However, if only a salt treatment is used to destroy parasites, it may be desirable to use an aquarium heater for the two-week period to heat the tank to 86 to 93 degrees Fahrenheit. The temperature should not be raised more than one degree per hour to avoid risking the fish. Such temperatures will kill most parasites. Following the treatment period, allow the tank water to cool back down to the pool temperature before transferring the fish.

Maintain good aeration during treatments. If the fish are affected by parasites, they may be weakened and have a greater need of oxygen. New fish should be observed for signs of skin lesions, raised scales, protruding eyes, open wounds, rapid breathing, white spots, frayed fins, skin or eye cloudiness, and scratching (flashing) behavior. If the fish continue to feed with the presence of symptoms, the problem is likely to be parasites. If the fish are not feeding, the problem is likely to be protozoan.

Never leave a fish in medicated water longer than is recommended. Never leave a fish unattended if it is immersed in short-term baths or

Falling leaves quickly sink to the pond bottom, where they rapidly begin decomposition that fouls your fish's winter water.
Photo by H. Nash

dips. Remove the fish immediately if it displays signs of great stress or attempts to jump from the bath.

Always disinfect nets between uses. The hospital tank should be thoroughly cleaned and disinfected after its use.

OPENING/CLEANING/ DRAINING THE POND

Even if the pond doesn't freeze over the winter, a spring cleaning ensures the health and well-being of the fish and plants. It is much less stressful on the fish if pond cleaning is done while they are still sluggish and the water is below 50 degrees Fahrenheit.

If you've maintained a regular pond-cleaning routine, you may not need to fully empty it. Instead, a simple 30-percent water exchange and thorough vacuuming of the pond bottom may be enough maintenance for the spring opening. If the pond doesn't have a bottom drain, use a submerged pump to remove the water.

During a complete pond cleaning, tending the fish is critical. They must be removed from the pond to a safe holding tank. Deep, narrow trash cans are too cramped and quickly stress any size fish. Use a child's wading pool at least eighteen inches deep, a livestock watering tank, or a portable koi show tank. If you use a new aluminum livestock tank, scrub it well with vinegar and rinse it several times to prevent the zinc from leaching out. Whatever you use, be sure it is clean and has an appropriate cover. Mesh netting or tulle fabric allows air to access the water surface for gas exchanges and, if secured properly over the container, safely prevents the fish from jumping out. Check that the cover does not have holes or gaps; if there's a hole, that's where a fish will jump. Dissolve one-half to one pound of non-iodized salt per 100 gallons of water as a stress tonic in the holding tank. Adding Stress Coat® helps, too. (If the fish have parasitic or fungal problems, figuring medication dosages is easiest if the holding tank is one foot deep.)

Use a submersible pump set in the pond to fill the holding tank with pond water. An aerator assures adequate oxygen in the tank. Most pet stores offer long bar stones that

provide the aeration of several smaller stones. These bars are also heavier and sink, while small stones tend to float in their bubbles at the surface.

Once your holding tank has been set up in a nearby shady location, you can move the fish. Lower the water level before you net them out. With less space in which to flee, they are easier to catch. If potted plants are in the pool, remove them to further ease fish removal. Set the pots in a shady site if the day is sunny. Cover sprouting water lilies with wet burlap or newspapers or submerge them in a bucket of water. Once the pond water has been drawn low, but with enough depth that the fish can still swim about without breaking the surface, you can net them. (If you must enter the pond, have a helper topside to move the fish on over to the holding tank.)

Use a net large enough to hold the largest fish without his lopping over the edge. Likewise, use a shallow net so the fish does not become entangled in the depths of it, catching and tearing off scales. Never handle any fish without first wetting your hands; this will protect their slime coating. To handle a large fish, place one hand over the head and eyes and, gently but firmly, lift the fish when you are sure you have it under control. Be single-minded about capturing your fish. Pick out one you will net and focus only on it. Do not swish the net wildly in the water; this will frighten the fish. Following winter hibernation, fish will have lost weight and will be more susceptible to infections and parasites; stress, too, increases the chance of such problems.

Before moving fish into the holding tank, hold the net at the surface and check for parasites and disease. Move the fish into the holding tank and secure the protective net. Check occasionally that they are not displaying signs of stress or oxygen deprivation (gasping at the surface).

With the pond water now quite low, don't let the pump run dry. If your pond was built with a slope to a deeper point or with a sump well, you won't have to mop up the last water with towels. Scrub down the sides of the pond and the bottom with a clean brush that has not been treated with chemicals or used with detergents or bleaches. Do not use any cleansers within the pond. Use fresh water from a hose to wash down the scrubbed areas, then remove the dirty water from the pool. Start refilling the pond and treat for chlorine, if necessary. Remember to check whether the water supply has chloramine. If the ammonia level in the fresh water is at fish-toxic levels, reduce it with an ammonia detoxifier, such as Amquel or Ammo Lock 2, before returning the fish to the pond. Always test the water before returning the fish to be sure it is safe.

As your pond fills, repot any plants that require roomier quarters. Give plants their first seasonal dosage of fertilizer, cutting it in half if the season is still early.

This is the time, too, to clean and set up the biofilter. Seed it with bacteria once it is in line and functioning. Even without a biofilter in the pond, once the water is completely free of chlorine, add nitrifying bacteria to jump-start the bio-system.

With the pond refilled and the water testing safe, compare the temperatures of the pond water and the holding tank. If there is more than a one-degree difference, acclimate the fish to the temperature change just as with new fish. Ease a fish or two into a large plastic bag filled with the tank water and float the bag on the pond's surface until the temperatures are equalized, or remove water from the holding tank a bucket or two at a time and replace it with an equal amount from the pond every 15 minutes until the temperatures equalize. Then move the fish directly by net.

Appendix

Ideas for Above-Ground Ponds

Use thick paving stones to create the walls, line the structure with pond membrane, and cap with thinner and wider stones to conceal the liner. Use a similar construction method around a preformed pond that is set upon the ground. Combine concrete construction with facing rocks of your choice.   Photo by H. Nash

Thread drilled landscape timbers onto long post-screws, log-cabin style.
Photo courtesy of Tetra Second Nature

Line the structure with plywood and a pond liner and cap with top edging. Finish the outside by filling in the alternating spaces with timbers cut to the inner dimensions.
Photo by H. Nash

Sawn timbers can be used for a more refined effect.   Photo by H. Nash

Make it easy on your-
self and use a kit.
Photo by H. Nash

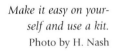

Match your deck construction to create a pond that fits between the deck and your above-ground swimming pool.
Photo by H. Nash

Use a shallow preformed pond to create a bog garden. Shown is Steve Stroupe's carnivorous plant garden. He cam-ouflages the pond form with a tasteful wooden enclosure.
Photo by H. Nash

Build a standing pond indoors for year-round enjoyment. Northern climates may need sup-plemental grow lights during the shorter days of winter for day-dependent tropical plants.
Photo by H. Nash

THE TUB GARDEN

Tub gardens offer solutions to questions of design and practicality. Used in the landscape just like terrestrial planters, they fill voids and provide accents. Practically, they fulfill the desire for a water garden when, for whatever reason, you can't dig a hole in the yard, or when young children cause you to put your "big pond" plans on hold...and, of course, tub gardens are the alternative to composting those extra pond plants!

The traditional tub garden is a whiskey barrel, which is capable of holding 80 gallons of water, a few small fish, and a selection of aquatic plants. The true whiskey barrel, however, must be lined to prevent leakage and to avoid alcohol residues or tannic acid from leaching into the water. Readily available premolded liners solve this problem, or you can line the tub with a double layer of 4 × 4' plastic or with a pond liner membrane. Two or three coats of neoprene paint properly seals such containers, too. Inexpensive plastic containers of comparable size are available at most building supply and garden centers, as are large terra cotta pots, which offer charming or elegant design possibilities. Seal terra cotta on the inside with a concrete sealer or spray urethane.

Setting Up a Tub Garden

Materials Needed
watertight container, appropriately sealed if necessary

(liner or plastic, if necessary)

props for plants (these can be concrete blocks, bricks, or free-standing shelf units)

plants

Optional:
small submersible pump, (up to 80 GPH)

small spouting ornament

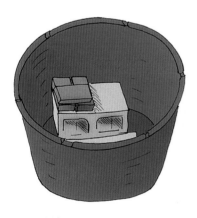

Seal any new concrete blocks if you will have fish in your tub garden. Blocks with holes in them provide support for plants without displacing too much water. The "tunnels" provide safe hiding for the fish, too! Use a combination of blocks and bricks to achieve proper depths for your plant selections.

Another option for creating varying water depths is the new "locker shelf" units now available in office supply stores. These open and lightweight metal units are coated with plastic. Available in black, they make perfect water garden shelf units!

Fill the tub with water, treating for chlorine if necessary. Add plants. After a few days, you may add two or three small fish. Spouting ornaments can be affixed to the side of the tub or set in a pot within the garden. Adjust the water flow with a clamp tightened no more than halfway on the tubing leading to the ornament.

Tub Gardening Tips

❧ If you won't include fish, use *Bt* in the form of floating doughnuts to control mosquitoes.

❧ Include submerged aquatic grasses to help control algae growth.

❧ Select small-growing fish such as hardy comet goldfish or a couple of the fancier goldfish varieties. Tropical fish often do well in container gardens since the garden is usually dismantled for winter anyway.

❧ If your summer weather is hot and the water temperature in your tub is likely to exceed 70 degrees Fahrenheit, consider siting the garden where temperatures won't be so high, or select fish that are happier with such temperatures. (Goldfish are cold-water fish.)

❧ The easiest way to deal with green-water episodes may be to change the water. If fish are present, take care to keep them from temperature changes and chlorinated water.

❧ Select plants in scale and growth habit suitable for the container.

Seal a terra cotta pot to keep an aquatic plant on the deck or patio.
Photo by H. Nash

Ideas for Container Gardens

Use containers for specimen aquatics to adorn the yard.   Photo by Ron Everhart

Black kettle planters make perfect containers for dwarf lotuses.   Photo by Bob Romar, courtesy of Maryland Aquatic Nurseries

A watertight wheelbarrow serves as a rustic, portable water garden.
Photo by H. Nash

Lined or sealed whiskey barrels hold an arrangement of marginal aquatic plants.
Photo by H. Nash

In France, a hanging pot holds a dwarf water lily. Photo by Eamonn Hughes

A Runestone Trough Container Water Garden with a Reservoir

To solve the problems sometimes encountered with container water gardens—evaporation, water temperature fluctuations, and green water—Carol Felsing and Richard Wright, owners of Pond Reflections in White Bear Lake, Minnesota, developed a unique container design using their own design of the traditional Runestone planting trough.

You will need:

1 watertight container. Theirs is 2 × 3 feet and 18 inches deep and has a 1½-inch hole in the bottom for the hose from the pump. You can also use a statue, bird bath, or grist mill stone.

1 hole in the ground at least one foot greater in diameter than the water feature splash area and about 1–3 feet deep with the deepest point to one side but not underneath the water feature.

2 cubic yards or enough washed river rock and gravel mixture to fill the reservoir.

1 oil-less, submersible, small pump. They use an 80 GPH.

Enough flexible black hose to move water from the pump to the water output in the container or feature. They used approximately 5 feet.

A 9-inch × 9-inch irrigation catch basin with 1–2 foot extension and cover grate. (If this is not available, a section of 9-inch-diameter plastic culvert can be used with a piece of hard plastic cut to fit over the top for a cover. Cut 4-inch holes in the sides at the base to attach the 4-inch drain pipe. Make the culvert approximately 6 inches lower than the rim of the reservoir.)

A 20-foot roll of 4-inch flexible, perforated drain field pipe (rigid pipe can be used but absolutely must have holes in it).

A small tube of aquarium silicon caulk.

1 EPDM liner of 45-mil thickness or more. Determine size by measuring the width of the hole plus the depth, multiply by 2, and add 2 more feet for extra.

Enough nylon carpet, liner pad, or half-inch thickness of newspapers to line the hole.

Electricity to the site.

Directions

After digging the hole, carefully remove all rocks and pebbles from the excavation and line the hole with padding and the liner membrane. Minimize run-off water from entering the reservoir if it might be polluted with fertilizer, weed spray, or sediment. Position the irrigation catch basin at the lowest point and attach the drain field pipe on at least three sides of the basin. The pipe should be curled around on the bottom of the reservoir and end caps put on the open ends. Install pump and inlet hose with clamps; if needed, cut a hole in the side of the irrigation basin for the inlet hose to go through. Put the cover in place. Next, gently add rocks, avoiding placement of any sharp edges next to the liner. Place your container over the reservoir, leaving room for access to the pump, and hook up to the outlet hose from the pump. If needed, use aquarium silicon to hold it in place.

Level the container and be sure it sits solidly on the reservoir rock. Add water and plug in the pump. Install a cover over the pump housing and a layer of rocks on top. Carol reports that in four years, she's never had to change the water. Topping the container off once a month is usually required. A fountain setup, however, would involve more evaporation. Even though the water level may be lowered in the reservoir through evaporation, the container is fed a constant level for fish and plants. With shade provided to the reservoir water, along with the steady earth temperature, there is less fluctuation within the container garden than is usually encountered. The rocks provide surfaces for bacterial colonization and bio-filtration. With the pump in the deepest part of the reservoir, taking its water from the pipes in the bottom minimizes pockets of anaerobic water.

The same type of plants used in any other small water garden can be used in the reservoir container. Hardy plants such as water iris or miniature cattails can be grown in the reservoir rocks, allowing plant roots to remain in water. These plants can be left in place through the winter. Carol notes that leaving a shallow spot in the container makes a handy birdbath, too.

The water inlet for Carol's container is located in the bottom of a Runestone trough container that she makes from a special concrete to resemble stone. When ice starts to form on the sides and top of the trough in their zone 4 winter, she unplugs the pump to allow all the water to drain out of the trough and back into the reservoir. A plywood lid covers the Runestone to keep out rain and snow that might freeze and break the trough. They leave the pump submerged below throughout the winter, keeping snow piled on top of the rocks over it for extra insulation.

Excavate the reservoir so that it slopes to one end.
Photo by Carol Felser

Lining the reservoir excavation with porous landscape fabric helps keep dirt from clogging the pipes.
Photo by Carol Felser

By recycling the water from a cool, hidden reservoir, your pond will always have clear water. Photo by Carol Felser

*I*deas for Creative Touches...

Moving the Water

*Mill houses and water wheels can be minia-
ture or full-sized.*
Photo by H. Nash

*Plumbing a pump to
recycle water from the
reservoir pond sends
the water into a
whiskey barrel plant
filter and into a
stream for its return to
the pond.*
Photo by H. Nash

*It takes time to drill through stone, but a
flowing rock may be worthwhile.*
Photo by H. Nash

A geyser fountain head creates another look. Vary it even more with glass balls over the reservoir. Photo by H. Nash

Set plumbed statuary within the pond waters. Photo by H. Nash

A dry stream bed makes an attractive pond overflow or drainage accommodation. Photo by H. Nash

Convert a fountain into a water garden.
Photo by M.J. Girot

Create a charming setting with a bird-bath or dish garden.   Photo by H. Nash

*Stepping stones add
interest to the garden.*
Photo by H. Nash

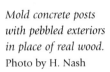

*Mold concrete posts
with pebbled exteriors
in place of real wood.*
Photo by H. Nash

*It's easy to fall in love with this antique
blue enamel stove...*   Photo by H. Nash

*...when extra floating
plants soon find their way
into pots on the stove.*
Photo by H. Nash

Displaying Art

Water need not flow over the waterfall....let it flow under a stone and display a statue.   Photo by H. Nash

A dragonfly sculpture poses in a pond at the National Wildflower Research Garden in Austin, Texas.
Photo by H. Nash

Adding Structures

The Aikins' pond echoes its gazebo
design in a matching bridge.
Photo by H. Nash

Bridges are always enticing.
Photo by Greg Jones

A small gazebo offers a shady resting place during the day and a quiet place to dine at night.   Photo by H. Nash

Build a pergola over the pond and train vines up its posts.
Photo by H. Nash

With proper reinforcement, you can make your own mold for a pebble-faced, concrete bridge span.   Photo by H. Nash

Even a small preformed pond can be part of a railroad garden.
Photo by H. Nash

This train detours into the house, to be loaded with fish food to dump into the pond via remote control. Photo by H. Nash

Many aquatic plants, such as this water forget-me-not (Myosotis palustris), will grow within gently flowing water. Photo by H. Nash

Plants for Streams and Vegetative Filters

Acorus calamus 'Variegata'—sweet-flag; height: 1–4', hardy to zone 4, blooms summer, sun

Acorus gramineus 'Variegata'—height: 9", hardy to zones 7–10, blooms spring/summer, sun

Butomus umbellatus—flowering rush; height: 3', hardy to zone 6, blooms spring/summer, sun

Calla palustris—bog arum; height: 1', hardy to zone 5, blooms spring/summer, shade

Caltha palustis—marsh marigold; height: 1', hardy to zone 5, blooms

Acorus calamus 'Variegata', *sweet flag*
Photo by H. Nash

spring/summer, shade

Cardamine cordifolia—heartleaved bittercress; height: 4"–32", hardy to zone 5, blooms early summer, shade to sun

Carex obnupta—slough sedge; height: 2', hardy to zone 4, blooms summer, sun

Cyperus alternifolius—umbrella palm; height: 3', hardy to zone 8, blooms summer, sun

Echinodorus cordifolia—radican sword; height: 2', hardy to zone 6, blooms summer, part shade

Eleocharis palustris—common spike rush; height: 1', hardy to zone 3, blooms spring, sun

Eriophorum angustifolium—cotton grass; height: 15", hardy to zone 4, blooms summer, sun

Houttuynia cordata—Houttuynia; height: 18", hardy to zone 5, blooms white in the summer, part shade

Houttuynia cordata 'Variegata'—chameleon plant; height: 18", hardy to zone 5, blooms summer, part shade

Hydrocotyle umbellata—pennywort; height: 1', hardy to zone 5, blooms summer, sun

Iris fulva—red iris; height: 1', hardy to zone 5, blooms spring, part shade

Iris pseudacorus—yellow flag iris; height: 3', hardy to zone 5, blooms spring, sun

Iris versicolor—blue flag iris; height: 18", hardy to zone 5, blooms late spring, part shade

Juncus effusus—soft rush; height: 2', hardy to zone 3, blooms summer, sun

Juncus ensifolius—dagger leaf rush; height: 1', hardy to zone 3, blooms summer, sun

Juncus patens—blue spreading rush; height: 18", hardy to zone 3, blooms summer, sun

Lysimmachia nummularia—creeping jenny; creeper, hardy to zone 4, blooms summer, part shade

Lysimmachia nummularia 'Aurea'—yellow-leafed creeping jenny; creeper, hardy to zone 4, blooms summer, sun

Menyanthes trifoliata—bog bean; height: 1', hardy to zone 5, blooms spring, part shade

Mimulus guttatus—yellow monkey flower; height: 1', hardy to zone 4, blooms summer, sun

Nasturtium officinale—watercress; creeper, hardy to zone 6, blooms spring/summer, part shade

Oenanthe—water celery; variety *javanica* 'Flamingo' has multicolored leaves; height: 12", hardy to

zone 5, blooms white in the summer, sun

Peltandra virginica—spoonflower; height: 2', hardy to zone 5, blooms summer, part shade

Pontederia cordata—purple pickerel weed; height: 20", hardy to zone 3, blooms late summer, sun

Ranunculus flammula—small creeping spearwort; height: 6", hardy to zone 3, blooms spring/summer, sun

Sagittaria latifolia—arrowhead; height: 2', hardy to zone 3, blooms summer, sun

Saururus cernuus—lizard tail; height: 2', hardy to zone 4, blooms summer, sun

Scirpus—bulrush; zebra rush; white rush; height: to 5', hardy to zone 3, blooms summer, part shade

Typha latifolia 'Variegata'—cattail; height 2 to 6', depending on variety, hardy to zone 3, blooms summer, sun

Typha latifolia *'Variegata'*
Photo by Ron Everhart

LIST OF COMMONLY AVAILABLE AQUATIC PLANTS
BY BOTANIC/COMMON NAME

Alligator weed	*Alternanthera ficoidea*
Amazon water lily	*Victoria amazonica*
Anacharis	*Egeria densa*
Arrow arum	*Peltandra virginica*

Arrowhead	*Sagittaria*
Arum lily	*Zantedeschia*
Banana lily	*Nymphoides aquatica*
Bladderwort	*Utricularia*
Blue bells	*Ruellia squarrosa*
Blue flag iris	*Iris versicolor*
Blue water hyacinth (rooting, nonbulbous)	*Eichhornia azurea*
Bog arum	*Calla palustris*
Bogbean	*Menyanthes trifoliata*
Bulrush	*Scirpus*
Butterwort	*Pinguicula*
Button bush	*Cephalanthus occidentalis*
Calla lily	*Zantedeschia*
Canadian pondweed	*Elodea canadensis*
Cardinal flower	*Lobelia cardinalis*
Cattail	*Typha*
Common reed	*Phragmites*
Coontail	*Ceratophyllum demersum*
Cotton grass	*Eriophorum angustifolium*
Creeping Jenny	*Lysimachia nummularia*
Curled pondweed	*Potamogeton crispus*
Duck potato	*Sagittaria latifolia*
Duckweed	*Lemna minor*
Dwarf sagittaria	*Sagittaria natans*
Fairy moss	*Azolla*
Flat-bladed rush	*Juncus macrophyullus*
Floating fern	*Ceratopteris pteridoides or C. thalictroides*
Floating heart	*Nymphoides peltata*

Lavender musk	*Mimulus ringens*
Lizard tail	*Saururus cernuus*
Loosestrife	*Lythrum salicaria*
Lotus	*Nelumbo*
Manna grass	*Glyceria*
Marsh marigold	*Caltha palustris*
Mediterranean rush	*Arundo donax*
Melon sword	*Echinodorus radican*
Monkey flower	*Mimulus*
Mosaic plant	*Ludwigia sedioides*
Orange snowflake	*Nymphoides hydrocharioides*
Papyrus	*Cyperus*
Parrot's feather	*Myriophyllum aquaticum*
Parrot leaf	*Alternanthera ficoidea*
Pennywort	*Hydrocotyle*
Pickerel weed	*Pontederia*
Pitcher plant	*Sarracenia*
Powdery thalia	*Thalia dealbata*
Prickly water lily	*Euryale ferox*
Red-stemmed thalia	*Thalia geniculata* form ruminoides
Rose mallow	*Hibiscus moschuetos*
Santa Cruz water lily	*Victoria cruziana*
Sensitive plant	*Neptunia aquatica, Aeschynomene fluitans*
Soft rush	*Juncus*
Southern blue flag iris	*Iris virginica*
Southern swamp lily	*Crinum americanum*
Spatterdock	*Nuphar advena, N. lutea*
Spearwort	*Ranunculus*
Spike rush	*Eleocharis*
Star grass	*Dichromena colorata*
Sundew	*Drosera*
Swamp hibiscus	*Hibiscus moschuetos*
Sweet flag	*Acorus calamus*

Flowering rush	*Butomus umbellatus*
Frogbit	*Hydrocharis morsus-ranae*
Giant water snowflake	*Nymphoides indica 'Gigantea'*
Golden club	*Orontium aquaticum*
Gorgon plant	*Euryale ferox*
Gray sedge	*Carex pseudocyperus*
Hair grass	*Eleocharis acicularis*
Horsetail rush	*Equisetum*
Ivy-leaf duckweed	*Lemna trisulca*
Japanese iris	*Iris ensata*

Tape grass	*Vallisneria*
Taro	*Colocasia*
Two-leaf clover	*Regnellidum diphyullum*
Umbrella palm	*Cyperus alternifolius*
Variegated rush	*Baumea rubiginosa*
Variegated Water snowflake	*Nymphoides cristatum*
Venus flytrap	*Dionaea*
Watercress	*Nasturtium officinale*
Water bamboo	*Dulichium arundinaceum*
Water chestnut	*Eleocharis tuberosa*
Water clover	*Marsilea*
Water fern	*Salvinia* or *Ceratopteris pteridoides,* or *C. thalictroides*
Water forget-me-not	*Myosotis palustris* and *M. scorpioides*
Water hawthorne	*Aponogeton distachyus*
Water hyacinth	*Eichhornia crassipes*
Water lettuce	*Pistia stratiotes*
Water meal	*Wolffia*
Water mint	*Mentha aquatica*
Water plantain	*Alisma plantago-aquatica*
Water poppy	*Hydrocleys nymphoides*
Water primrose	*Ludwigia peploides*
Water soldier	*Stratiotes aloides*
Water spider lily	*Hymenocallis liriosme*
Water spinach	*Ipomea batatas*
White rush	*Scirpus lacustris* 'Albescens'
Wild rice	*Zizania latifolia*
Woolgrass	*Scirpus cyperinus*
Yellow flag iris	*Iris pseudacorus*
Yellow fringe	*Nymphoides geminata*
Yellow pond lily	*Nuphar sp.*
Zebra rush	*Scirpus lacustris* ssp. *tabernaemontani*

SHADE-TOLERANT WATER PLANTS

Water Lilies

Most blue tropicals, especially 'Director George T. Moore' and 'Isabella Pring', a white

Hardies: 'James Brydon,' 'Masaniello,' 'Lucida,' 'Hal Miller,' 'Chromatella,' 'Attraction,' 'Escarboucle,' 'Froebeli,' 'Comanche,' 'Paul Hariot,' 'Chrysantha'

Marginal Aquatic Plants

Parrot's feather, Cabomba, non-flowering marginals

ACKNOWLEDGMENTS

$\mathcal{T}$his book would not have been possible if not for the sharing of information and experiences of hundreds of people over the past 10 years, from dear friends in the industry to warm souls who shared their gardens with us. Nor would this book have happened if Sheila Anne Barry, acquisitions manager at Sterling Publishing Company, had not asked, "Helen, which one of your books would you recommend for the beginner water gardener?"

We owe a special thank you to Tavo and Chic Kelty of Santa Fe Water Gardens in Santa Fe, New Mexico, for sharing their information on filtration, a sorely neglected topic in print.

Also, in producing a magazine, we have gained a new respect for the behind-the-scenes efforts of editors and technical artists. This appreciation prompts warm kudos for the work of our editor, Hannah Steinmetz, and our graphic designer, Judy Morgan.

Thank you all!

METRIC CONVERSIONS

Mathematics of Conversions

To convert	Multiply by	To obtain
inches	2.54	centimeters
inches	25.4	millimeters
feet	30	centimeters
pounds	0.45	kilograms
U.S. gallons	3.8	liters

Fahrenheit to Celsius: Subtract 32, multiply by 5, and divide by 9.

INDEX

Boldface type indicates artwork